EVERYDAY MIRACLES

Moments of Healing and Transformation

Edited by Kendra Langeteig
Copyright © 2016 Quiet Fire Press
ISBN-13: 978-0692808894

**Quiet Fire
Press**

P.O Box 29258
Bellingham, WA 98228
Book Design and Typesetting by Rod Burton
Illustrations by Stephanie Strong
Cover photos by Rosemary DeLucco Alpert

All things are possible ... only believe

Dear Readers:

We invite you to enjoy this collection of our favorite "miracle" stories. The original true stories that we share with you in this book are published here for the first time. Our storytellers are seasoned travelers who've walked through the proverbial fire to discover who they are and what is possible in life when guided by spirit. The stories were generously contributed by many of the "wisdom keepers" at the Unity Spiritual Center in Bellingham, Washington, including minister Bob Trask, whose storytelling is legendary.

The miracles in this book come in all shapes and sizes. Some of them are awe-inspiring. You will read about astonishing recoveries from life-threatening illness, spontaneous healing from seemingly incurable disease, and safe passage through dangerous war zones. You will also get a glimpse of the "other side" with accounts of near-death and out-of-body experiences, visits from angels, and messages received from departed loved ones. Miracles arise as well from a sudden shift in perception, a moment of grace that forever changes someone's life. There are stories about the joy of finding true love, reuniting with lost birth family, taking the long spiritual journey home to Unity, and many more.

The authors of **Everyday Miracles** emphasize the importance of listening to our inner voice for guidance. They also show the importance of listening to the body's wisdom to guide the healing process and make choices in life. You will see convincing evidence in many of these stories of the power of positive thinking. You will also get insight into how intuitive healers work with subtle energy and access information from spirit guides. There is much to learn from the collective wisdom shared in this unique book.

We hope that our stories will touch your heart and inspire you to be a miracle worker in your own life.

Many blessings,

The Editor, Kendra Langeteig, and the Contributors

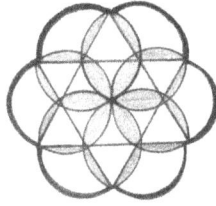

Contents

Chapter 1   **Trusting Spirit to Guide the Way**

Peg Rashband, *Flying on Course* — 13

Penny Sanford, *Staying Calm in the Middle of Chaos* — 16

Dac Jamison, *Unconscious Creation* — 19

Russ Kapp, *Riders on the Storm* — 25

Chapter 2   **Transforming the Way We See**

Ellen Kastler, *Beyond the Uniform* — 33

Ross Osborne, *The Miracle of Forgiveness* — 40

Kathy Chasteen, *Celebrate Yourself* — 42

Joyce Jones, *This is My Life and I'm Going to Live It* — 46

Chapter 3   **Creating Our Reality**

Ross Osborne, *How Changing My Thinking about Money Changed My Life* — 55

Jonathan Hall, *The Choices We Make* — 58

Maureen Hofstedt, *I'm Here to Tell the Tale* — 61

Mary Trask, *Ask and You Receive* — 64

Larry Harriman, *The Way Life Is Supposed to Be* — 66

Chapter 4   **Healing Is Believing**

Russ Eiriksson, *Going Back to the Basics* — 75

Larry Harriman, *The Wise Doctor* — 78

RoseMarie Longmire, *My Path to Wholeness* — 81

Helga DeLiban, *Healing Power of Love* — 83

Chapter 5 **Miracles of Healing**

Jon Strong, *The New Bob* 87

Maureen Hofstedt, *Angels Watching Over Me* 92

Christa Armstrong, *The Miracle Baby* 95

Elly Morrison, *Memories from a Hamburg Townhouse* 98

Polly Richter, *The Heavenly Helper* 102

Chapter 6 **Divine Timing – *Signs & Synchronicities***

Kathy Chasteen, *Trust God to Give You a Sign* 107

Bill Hamar, *The Green Card* 111

Shari Humes, *Somewhere in Time – A Love Story* 114

John Logan, *The Answer to a Prayer* 120

Chapter 7 **Unexpected Gifts**

Jon Strong, *Little Things* (poem) 125

Kelly Jamison, *A Gift from Grandma* 126

Erin O'Reilly, *Listening with Your Heart* 131

Sally Ledgerwood, *A Final Gift of Words* 133

Bell Spence, *Brotherly Love* 136

Chapter 8 **Blessings at Heaven's Door**

Marcia Reimers, *A Song for Mom* 141

Beatrice Raymond, *There Are Many Mansions* 145

Judy Milton, *First a Good-bye, Then a Hello* 148

Kendra Langeteig, *'Til Death Do Us Part* 150

Chapter 9 **Between Heaven and Earth –**
**   *Life Beyond the Veil***

Zella Chapman, The Day I Went to Heaven 159

Emma Jones, *The Keepers of the Scrolls* 162

Bruce Hofstetter, *Sailing with an Angel* 167

Zella Chapman, *Victor Street Ghost* 171

Muriel Crusciola, *Mike's Idea of Heaven* 173

Chapter 10 **Affirmation & Meditation**

Moira Haagen, *Healing Grace*   177

Polly Richter, *My Heart Is Your Heart*   181

Neal Engelking, *My Secret for Instant Bliss*   185

Jon Strong, *Nightly Affirmation*   188

Chapter 11 **Many Paths to Unity**

Alita Walton, *Remembering Who I Am*   193

Jonathan Hall, *The Impossible Takes a Little Longer* 197

Aaron Buhler, *Experiencing Unity*   200

RoseMarie Longmire, *Finding My Way Back Home*   202

George Rounthwaite, *The Deeps You Cannot See*   205

Chapter 12 **Miracle Workers**

Bob Trask, *My Mom, the Healer*   213

Christina Lorraine, *With These Hands*   216

Emma Jones, *Birth Family—The Inner Library*   222

Richard Morrison, *Listening to the Body's Wisdom*   225

About the Contributors   232

Chapter 1

Trusting Spirit
to Guide the Way

Everyday Miracles

Flying on Course

As a child I became interested the idea of flight. It seemed to me to personify true freedom—freedom from the earth, gravity, and all physical encumbrances. I loved birds on the wing exuding joy, ease, and apparent effortless grace. This interest in flying led me to put in many hours of study and practice towards becoming a licensed pilot.

When flying a plane, the compass is one of the most important instruments in the cockpit. The wise pilot keeps a constant check on the direction the plane is flying relative to the planned destination. Any slight movements off course are immediately corrected if the pilot doesn't wish to deal with out-of-control situations! This is also a metaphor for navigating through life situations and choice points regardless of desired goals and/or achievements.

As a young and green student pilot, I planned a cross-country flight from the metro area of Utah, which included my home base at Salt Lake International Airport, to a small remote town 120 miles away. A potential pilot must complete several solo flights in order to obtain a license.

I was flying near eight-to ten-thousand-foot mountains, part of the Rocky Mountain chain, which can be quite dangerous, depending on wind direction and speed, creating downdrafts that can pull a plane onto the mountain in one fell swoop.

I plotted my course, filed a flight plan, checked over the plane, and took off on a clear and mild summer morning. The view from 1000 feet above ground level was breathtaking as always—and I loved the feeling of perfect freedom!

About 40 minutes after takeoff, I took my attention off the instrument panel for the briefest of moments (it was only a second, I swear.) Looking up and around, it took me less than a minute to determine that I was not on my originally planned flight path. My skills were limited enough at the time that I didn't know how to get back on course. I figured that even if I corrected to the original compass heading, it wouldn't be enough to find my way, due to natural drift that occurs over time, which I didn't know how to correct for on the fly (no pun intended). Yikes! I was lost!

Pulling peace from deep within kept me calm and allowed me to focus on emergency protocol. I immediately began an intense sweep of the landscape, noting any areas suitable for emergency landings. Next, I looked for roads and railroad tracks that might lead to a town or city in what appeared to be a desolate, remote high desert area. After a few minutes, I began communicating "Mayday" via radio.

It felt like hours but was probably only 30 minutes or so when I "lucked out"! A voice came over the radio with great news; there was a small airport within a short distance. I reset the transponder and followed the voice and radar signal for a safe, albeit knee knocking, landing. At the Roosevelt Airport (out in the middle of nowhere), the traffic controller helped me flesh out an alternative flight plan, and within the hour I was off again into the wild blue yonder.

Everything went like clockwork, because I paid total and complete attention and made minute corrections as needed. What a big lesson! I never made the mistake of taking my mind off airborne business again. It was extremely difficult and risky to get back on track.

I have learned to apply this principle to my every day life with success, depending on the degree of vigilance I maintain. By checking in with my personal guidance system (inner truth or inner compass), which is intentionally aligned with the greater good, I manage to achieve some good and stay on path. That God works in mysterious ways is an understatement. God's love and help are available in any situation as long as you open yourself to tune in and receive! And, of course, pay attention.

—Peg Rashband

Staying Calm
in the Middle of the Chaos

On November 1, 2013, I flew from Seattle to Phoenix for a continuing education course. I left SeaTac Airport in the morning and had an hour-and-a-half layover at LAX. Our morning flight left Seattle on time and landed on schedule. While we were in the air, a shooting took place at LAX that killed one TSA officer and injured several others. The shooting shut down the majority of the air traffic, however, we landed at the airport uninformed as to what was happening. I exited the plane and could tell immediately that something major in the world had occurred. All the TVs in the area were on the same channel and everyone was watching the news, even the employees. I thought our president had been shot, but soon discovered this was a little closer to me. The event unfolding was at the airport I was standing in! From the news channel, I learned that Terminal 3 was completely shut down and virtually no one was able to enter or exit the airport.

I went over to look at the departure listings and saw that my flight was one of only a handful that were still listed as "on schedule." My connecting gate was close to where I had deplaned so I decided to sit down, relax, and meditate. I was going to a one-day course to prep for my Craniosacral Therapy practical exam. I was qualified to take it and had already passed the open-book essay, but did not feel competent enough with my skills to try the practical. I was on a fast track attempting to do this in less than 2 years time. If I didn't make this flight, I did not see any way I could get to the class, because according to the TV news, nobody was able to leave the airport parking lot or rent a car. The only purpose of my trip was to go to my class, so a cancelled flight could be waste of time and money as well. I sat there and visualized myself taking off on my connecting plane as scheduled multiple times. I also said to the Universe, "If I am meant to take this practical exam, please enable me to get to Phoenix."

I stayed close to my gate, had something to eat, watched as security personnel and dogs checked out all the people in the area. Time passed by and no sign of my connecting plane. Our scheduled "boarding time" had now passed and still, no plane. I sat and meditated some more. Then, about 20 minutes after we were supposed to start boarding, our plane arrived! Five minutes later, a pilot and crewmember went out to the plane and we heard the announcement: "Now boarding all passengers to Phoenix." I jumped up and got in a very short line to board my plane. Almost as soon as I was in my seat, the plane began to back away from the gate. I was in the back of the plane so I was able to do a head count: 10 people. We took off 5 minutes ahead of schedule on our flight to Phoenix. It was a pleasant, calm flight.

Midway to Phoenix, I asked the flight attendant, "How many people were supposed to be on this flight?" Her answer confirmed what I had suspected, "This was a fully booked flight and I am surprised that we were even able to land at LAX. Our departure out of San Diego was delayed for 1 hour because of the shooting and most of the planes were diverted to other local airports. Somehow we were given approval to land and take off at LAX. We are very excited because we are all heading home after a very long day." I realized then that the only people on the plane were those from my original flight out of SeaTac earlier in the day. We were the only passengers who could get to the gate because we landed only two gates away. I thanked the Universe and felt great gratitude as we landed in Phoenix on schedule. My trip had been unaffected by the chaos going on all around us. A little confirmation of this came when I was in line to rent a car a few minutes later. I noticed two fellow passengers in front of me and commented how amazing it was to have made it to Phoenix like we did with everything going on at LAX. A puzzled look appeared on both their faces. "Was there something going on at LAX?" they asked.

I took my class the next day and was encouraged to sign up for my practical exam at the end of the day. With the information I learned in the class and 3 weeks of focused practice, I felt prepared. I passed my exam the following month.

—*Penny Sanford*

Unconscious Creation

Stepping off the plane at Tan Son Nhut Air Base in Vietnam (Vietnamese: *Căn cứ không quân Tân Sơn Nhứt*) was my first experience in a foreign country. I had been to northern Mexico many times in college, but always just across the border to Ciudad de Juárez. I had also been to Canada. I figured neither of these experiences really counted.

On arrival in Vietnam, getting off the plane quickly was something I really wanted to do. After two aircraft breakdowns (Hawaii and Guam) and twenty-six hours in flight with hundreds of other GIs, the plane was very ripe.

The first thing that left an impression on me was the 120-degree heat pounding off the runway. The second thing was the assault of smells swarming in the air. JP4 (military jet fuel), rotting vegetation, hydraulic fluid, diesel fuel burning with human waste in cut-down 55-gallon drums, and a hundred other aromas were mixed into an alarmingly potent blend. The sweating GI smell in the plane was mild by comparison.

My third impression was of a large city of some beauty (Saigon) with masses of people. Most of the Vietnamese were dressed in bright or white colors, and walking or riding bicycles, scooters, motorcycles, and pedicabs—three-wheeled vans that were dancing in a slow motion, chaotic ballet. Traveling in a 2½-ton army truck (deuce and a half) through the streets gave me a great view of where I had been, but no clue of where I was going. After what seemed like hours sweltering in the rear of the truck, we arrived in the Bien Hoa Air Base/Replacement Depot.

Set out in military precision were row after row of barracks. They were very much like the WW II models in which I had taken Advanced Individual Training (AIT) at Fort Dix, New Jersey, except these had only screens where there should have been windows. The airbase next to the barracks was a pretty steady source of noise with jets, C-130 (Hercules), C-123 (Provider) and C-7 (Caribou) cargo planes taking off and landing twenty-four hours a day.

My first job in Vietnam was trying to cut mature bamboo with a dull machete. The bamboo had been allowed to grow right up to the perimeter fence. A few days before I arrived, the Viet Cong had attacked Bien Hoa Repo Depot. Because they were able to crawl right up to the wire unnoticed, they managed to kill a bunch of unarmed replacements housed there. A group of about fifty of us were sent outside the wire to chop at the overgrown bamboo. It was highly unrewarding work and it left our hands blistered and bruised. At the end of sixteen hours we had made some progress in opening fields of fire.

During the three days I spent at Bien Hoa, dozens of deuce and a halfs were filled with GIs headed to the field. It was the middle of Tet (Vietnamese New Year) in 1968, when the Viet Cong had launched many attacks and U.S. casualties were high. Many soldiers were taken to the field outside their Military Occupational Specialty (MOS), so cooks, wire men, and clerks became 11 Bravos (Infantry rifleman) in an instant, without the benefit of advanced infantry training.

On the fourth day in the country, I received orders to report to 44th Medical Brigade in Qui Nhon, a city on the ocean in II Corp area of operations. Two deuce and a halfs were waiting to take a bunch of us to the neighboring airbase and then we were loaded onto a C-130 cargo plane for the trip north. We flew to Pleiku, losing one engine on the way there. We then headed southeast to Qui Nhon, but the plane had trouble with a second engine on the way there, and had to divert to Cam Ranh Bay. The runway at Qui Nhon was too short to land on with only two engines to be able to reverse with.

When we arrived we were taken to a large hanger where there were hundreds of GIs bedded down on the cement floor. We found open spots and flopped down on the floor with our duffle bags as pillows. When I went to sleep, I was surrounded by GIs; when I awoke, I was almost alone in the hanger. The Army had conditioned me to sleep deeply at any opportunity, so I had missed all the activity when the hanger emptied out. I am sure someone had tried to wake me without success. I am also sure I was very rude to whoever tried, but I have no memory of that event. My wife still freaks out when she comes to pick me up somewhere and finds me standing up against a wall, asleep.

I remember thinking I was in serious trouble for having missed my flight, and I had no idea where I was in relation to Qui Nhon. My orders were to be in Qui Nhon that day and I had no way of getting there. It always amazes me how easy it is to have those lost little boy feelings.

There were two Air Force enlisted personnel behind a counter at the far end of the hangar who were very kind. I showed them my orders and they told me to go to the building next door.

They told me there was a general's plane leaving in a few hours for Qui Nhon and there was room on it for me. I sat on a bench in the shade until one of the Air Force guys came to get me. He led me to a twin engine Beechcraft King Air with Army markings on it. I was the last on board with my duffle bag in hand. Some high-ranking officers were up front, so I grabbed a seat in back. I was a smelly (no shower in three days) Private First Class, so I made myself as small as possible to avoid the officers' notice. I had worried needlessly, as they all seemed to be napping as we took off.

The plane was a huge upgrade from a C-130; the seat was first class. The trip was short and uneventful. I was left on the tarmac at Qui Nhon, the officers jumped into a waiting jeep and the plane taxied away. A short time later, a jeep with two Air Force enlisted men was driving by, and I flagged them down and they were accommodating. I asked them how to get to the 44th Med Brigade. They told to jump in and drove me there. It was a very good thing they did, as I don't think I would have found it on my own. I still have fondness for Air Force personnel.

As I arrived in the jeep I recognized some of the GIs that were on the C-130 with me getting into a deuce and a half, which left in the direction away from the 44th Med. HQ. The Air Force guys directed me to a Quonset hut surrounded with sand-filled 55-gallon drums topped with rows of sand bags. There were six Army clerks at desks inside the hut. I handed my orders and files to one of them. He looked over my files and asked me if I knew anything about radios. I confessed I knew nothing about radios; he said, "Great," and cut a set of orders for me. He told me to report to the building next door with the bunker attached to it.

When I arrived at the building, I got a quick tour and was

assigned a room in a newly built barracks. I was introduced to the water trailers, one was potable water for filling our canteens, and the other was non-potable water, which was used for filling our helmets for washcloth baths and shaving.

The next day I started OJT (on the job training) at 0600 hrs. I became a Radio Telephone Operator for the Medical Regulators in the 44th Medical Brigade. Our job was to take a of list casualties from the field and inform the 71st and 69th Evac Hospitals what medical patients they had coming in by helicopter. They were prepared with surgical teams ready when the patients arrived. We got the lists from Medical Regulators at the point the wounded were triaged and from Medical Evacuation Helicopters ("dustoffs") bringing them in from the field. We had FM radios and Collins single side-band long-range radios in the bunker. I was The FNG (unflattering Army jargon for a new person) in the unit so I worked mostly night shifts at first.

The 44th Med. Brig. was in charge of the Dust-off (helicopter evacuation) system in II Corp area. The bravery of the Dust-off pilots and crews was amazing. We were able to listen to the conversations between the embattled troops and the Dust-off during operations; exceptional bravery was common among the Dustoff pilots and crews. I flew on a few medevacs that were fairly routine; although in one I watched a Special Forces soldier die while I was sitting next to him in the hell-hole (side seat) of a Dustoff helicopter.

The medical evacuation system was pretty good because 96% of the wounded that were picked up and arrived alive at the Evacuation Hospitals survived. Because of the Dustoffs many boys who would have died survived because they arrived at hospitals much more quickly than the soldiers in WWII or Korea. The doctors and

nurses at the Evacuation Hospitals were the best. It was a little like
Mash 4077th but with better facilities, doctors, and nurses.

I was promoted twice to be in charge of radio communications with the Dust-off units after about nine months. I had to fly
all over II Corp to keep the radio net running. Most of the time I
flew by Dustoff Huey's (Army Iroquois Helicopters). I also flew in
Chinook helicopters, C-130, C-123, and C-7 cargo planes. I even
took a land convoy from Kontom in the central highlands to Qui
Nhon on the coast. I spent time at fire bases sleeping in Army tents.
I traveled from Dak To on the Laotian border to the coast well
south of Qui Nhon. The VC tried to blow me up at a hospital in
Pleiku, but I am sure it was not personal, it was just war. I had only
one close friend die the fifteen months I was there. Except for the
Evacuation Hospitals and staff of nurses and doctors, everything
in Vietnam was FUBAR (a military term for messed up badly).

I thought because of the Army enhancing my ability to sleep
well in any situation, I survived Tet of '68 and fourteen more
months in country. Although I knew nothing about the creative
power of the mind at the time, some part of me was making choices that had a good outcome for me.

In 1980 I took some personal growth classes and discovered
that I had always been very involved in the creation of my reality,
even if it seemed accidental. This was very good news and bad
news at the same time. When things went well, it was good indeed.
When things went badly, I now had to hold myself accountable for
that creation as well.

Co-creating my reality really has become a full-time job!

—*Dac Jamison*

Riders on the Storm

Coming from a childhood where I literally worshipped the high seas and the spirit of adventure and exploration, it was no surprise that I would enlist in the U.S. Navy during the Cold War years and the unfolding war in Vietnam. Following the Navy's extensive schooling and training in the electronics technician field, I became a Communications Technician (equipment maintenance branch) with a top-secret crypto clearance. My first duty station was aboard the USS Palm Beach (AGER-3). I was aboard the Palm Beach for both of its two major cruises overseas; the first being a deployment above the Arctic Circle region and the second cruise consisting of a deployment into the Mediterranean Sea joining the U.S. Navy's 6th fleet. The USS Palm Beach was commonly known as a "spy ship." As some might remember, our sister ship, the USS Pueblo, made headlines when it was captured by the North Koreans back in January of 1968. Our ships were nearly identical and our missions and operations were much the same. I was responsible for the repair and maintenance of our ship's radio, radar, and top-secret crypto gear, including teletypes and various specialized tape recorders.

The Palm Beach was originally built during WWII and was designed to transport and deliver Army Air Corps aircraft spare-parts to military bases along the western and eastern seaboards of the U.S. It was designated as a "light cargo/freighter" meant to hug coastlines and harbors. The Palm Beach along with its sister ships, the USS Banner and the USS Pueblo, were re-commissioned and converted into electronic surveillance vessels in the late 60's. All three ships were not much bigger than harbor fleet tugs and were never intended by their designers and contractors to be used as trans-oceanic vessels for any purpose. Yet, sail the Atlantic Ocean and the Mediterranean the Palm Beach did.

I sailed during the first Palm Beach cruise during the summer of 1968 along the Norwegian coast and above the Arctic Circle. The following spring of 1969 the USS Palm Beach was slated for a Mediterranean cruise. This second cruise had been scheduled to conclude sometime during the early days of July 1969. However, that plan was revised during the final few days of June, and for reasons never explained to me or the ship's company, the mission was extended through the better part of July. Little did I realize what that change in orders and strategy would mean for the trans-oceanic trip back to the Palm Beach's homeport in Norfolk, Virginia.

Looming on the horizon was the Atlantic Ocean's summer hurricane season of 1969. That year was later put on the record as the Atlantic Ocean's season with the highest number of tropical storms and hurricane systems since 1933. The Palm Beach's orders to extend the mission-stay on post in the Mediterranean Sea for another two weeks placed our return stateside such that we were bound to cross at least one seasonal U.S. East coast tropical storm, if not one of the early seasonal hurricanes. Few, if any, of us, were prepared for what was about to unfold the last few days of seafaring in late July going into early August of 1969.

A tropical wave from the West coast of Africa on July 23, 1969 had developed into tropical depression #12 by July 25th. On July 27th it was upgraded to tropical storm status—Anna. By July 29th Anna peaked with a maximum sustained wind speed of 65 mph as it tracked up the East coast from Florida upward through the mid-Atlantic latitudes. Within the week and on the heels of Anna was the first seasonal hurricane—Blanche. It was clocking-in with sustained wind speeds of 85 mph as it followed a similar trajectory as Anna up the eastern seaboard. Any sea-going vessel under this sort of threat is strongly urged to seek out any port—ASAP.

I recall the ensuing encounter with tropical storm Anna and hurricane Blanche commencing while the Palm Beach was yet some 300 to 500 nautical miles from the U.S. The violent nature of sustained horizontal wind speeds at 75 mph took minimal time to produce huge rolling swells on the order of 20-30 feet, each frequently towering and breaking over the Palm Beach's weather deck and associated rigging. It was a good two to three days of massive ocean waves repeatedly crashing over the ship; washing over the brink anything loose that was topside. I could feel the ship swaying wildly upwards of 45 degrees from side-to-side—port then starboard and back again. Looking out the below-deck port hole in forward berthing, all I could see for hours was occasional grey skies and streaming rain, interrupted by repeated underwater "Sea World" panoramas with each rolling ocean swell.

I imagined it was nature's version of a sinister ballroom dance from hell. I remember trying to hang on to anything solid as I attempted to move about the ship as it heaved between cresting-swells and plunging into the following troughs. Over and over, I could actually feel the USS Palm Beach sailing backwards while it repeatedly pitched, rolled and slammed itself violently into the next massive swell or wall of seawater. I thought to myself as I cinched down on the straps that secured me in my bunk bed for a few hours of sleep, my mother's water broke—I was born in the sign of water—I was baptized with water—I am about to die in the water—at least it won't be "dust-to-dust" for me. Such were the ironies of life.

By the beginning of the second day of this ongoing maelstrom, my stomach was growling with hunger. Things had escalated within hours to the point where it was necessary to cease all meals. The ship's mess deck was shut down. It was crackers and water if I was lucky enough to even crawl my way back to the galley for sustenance. Using the ship's forward berthing bathroom became for me something akin to a menacing clown routine from the Circus of Horrors. With every effort to make eye contact with my fellow crewmates, I frequently saw the look of terror written on each face. I wondered if we were all asking the same question, Could this next swell coming up be the last? At least I had enough common sense to realize the odds were clearly stacked against the Palm Beach ever making landfall.

I've never been much of a rote-praying person even in times of extreme trouble and emergencies. I never really believed there was a supreme Sky-Being running the show down here. However, by nightfall of the second day, there was a defining moment when I had lost all faith and nothing was left but the stark reality of eventually drowning in the turbulence. Why the USS Palm Beach hadn't broken in half or capsized was beyond me. If there was a prayer this time, it was one of a simple acceptance, so be it. Suddenly, I not only felt peace—*I was peace.*

With the storm's eventual subsiding three days after all hell broke loose, and blue skies developing once again overhead, life aboard the USS Palm Beach slowly returned to some semblance of order and balance. Landfall never looked so good to me and the crew upon our slow arrival into our Little Creek Norfolk, Virginia, Naval Base. Our little U.S. Navy intelligence-gathering ship was still rattled, but miraculously homebound. Later, I figured this cruise must have been some sort of intelligence gathering from a source that knows only love and grace.

—Russ Kapp

Chapter 2

Transforming the Way We See

Everyday Miracles

Beyond the Uniform

In the early morning hours of April 9, 1940, my world as I knew it was turned completely upside down. Tremendously loud noises came from outside. As we looked out the window, we saw hundreds of planes in the sky. The next thing we heard were loud speakers blaring with the urgent message to evacuate immediately. Oslo was going to be bombed by the Germans.

I was 12 years old and just getting ready for school. Plans drastically changed. My mother, Jenny Bergh, ordered me and my sister to dress extra warm and put on heavy boots. As we ran outside, we were met by our neighbors and immediately began working together to organize transportation to evacuate to the woods.

Fortunately, we were able to find someone with a car. It was small but we filled it with as many people as possible and headed north to the woods still blanketed with the winter's snow. There we waited and walked around for hours. Nothing seemed to be happening so we eventually decided to walk home. When we arrived, we immediately turned on the radio and listened as the announcer instructed the Norwegian people to return to our "normal life."

Within a few days, our town was full of German soldiers identified by unmistakable helmets and daunting swastikas on their arms. Hitler's army now officially occupied Norway. They said they were there to save us. Save us from what I wondered. What were they thinking?

The soldiers were everywhere, in shops, in restaurants, in grocery stores. They were buying food and supplies at an alarming rate. I remember watching German soldiers put a cube of butter between two chocolate bars. I thought this was odd at the time but looking back, I realized they were probably very hungry.

Many schools were taken over by the German soldiers and converted into living quarters. This forced us to share the building and attend school in the late afternoons and evenings. One day a new girl from Prague, Czechoslovakia came to my class. She had beautiful dark hair and somehow I knew she was Jewish. We would walk home from school together. On one of those days, two German soldiers were approaching us. Realizing that she could be in extreme danger, I walked in front of her trying to cover her up and hide her. Fortunately, they were so busy talking, they didn't notice us. I was so relieved that we had avoided a possible grave situation.

Going on public transportation was a risk. If you were riding a streetcar and a German soldier sat down next to you, you could be arrested if you stood up and remained standing as this was a sign of defiance. Often the curfew was after 8:00 pm. Anyone found on the street after that was shot and killed instantly.

In the year 1944, there was lovely Christmas play in downtown Oslo that I wanted to see. There was a 10-year-old girl that lived in the same four-plex, so we made plans to go to the play together. Right in middle of the performance, we heard some extremely loud noises. At first, I thought it was part of the play.

Everyone started to run out of the theatre and it was then that I realized the loud noises we had heard were actually explosions. I grabbed the little girl by the hand and we ran as fast as we could for a half hour to get home. Our mothers had been very nervous and were happy when we arrived home safely. Later I learned the explosions we heard were from Norwegian saboteurs blowing up German ammunition ships in the nearby harbor.

The borders were closed and the fjords were blocked so ships could not deliver supplies. Before long, all food and essential living provisions were in short supply and we became more and more desperate for food. It was impossible to buy new clothes. However, thanks to my mother's sewing skills, she made blouses and skirts for us out of old sheets. My feet were growing and I desperately needed larger shoes, but there were no shoes available to purchase. I remember somebody making shoes with wooden soles and fish skin for leather. As soon as they were worn in the rain, they fell apart.

My father, Honor Bergh, would take a train for several hours to his cousin's farmhouse. He took his life in his own hands by bringing food back to us in a backpack. If the train had been searched, he would have at least been arrested.

My mother got up at 5:00 every morning and waited in line until 9:00 a.m. in all kinds of weather hoping to get some food on our ration cards. At times there was nothing to buy.

We had some potatoes stored in the cellar. Without them we would have starved. I often went to bed very hungry.

By 1944 food was so scarce that my father took me out of school and sent me to a farm where he had arranged for me to stay for a while to get proper nourishment. We didn't know that the farmer, Christian Brinck, and his wife, Astrid, were storing an arsenal of weapons in their barn to supply the Norwegian resistance. We didn't know that one of Christian's employees would betray him and alert the Gestapo about the stored weapons.

The next morning, a truck filled with 150 German soldiers pulled up to the house. I was still asleep when bullets ripped through the wooden door of the bedroom I was sharing with a younger girl. Immediately I pulled her out of bed and onto the floor and began to pray.

The next thing I knew, the door was kicked open by a Nazi in full uniform. He put his gun up to my back and ordered me to go to the barn and look for Christian. I hurried and got dressed and walked through the snow and out to the barn and began calling his name. I soon found him sitting down and bleeding from his stomach. He had been shot during the attack at the house and had run out to the barn in hopes to escape. I was able to load him onto the sled and pull him up to the house. Once there, I saw that Astrid had been shot in the arm. Since the Geneva Convention stated that you could not kill a wounded enemy, the Nazis sent Christian and Astrid to the hospital to be healed before their execution. It was actually a well-known, skilled German doctor that operated on Christian and saved his life.

It wasn't long before the house, especially the kitchen, was crowded with German soldiers. I had just finished three years of German in school and had no problem with the language. The officer in charge told me to make soup for them. I wasn't about to serve the enemy, so I told him I didn't know how to cook, even though I did.

Soon the Germans began peeling potatoes for the soup. As

I watched, I turned to one of the soldiers and asked him, "You don't think you are really going to win the war the way you treat people, do you?" He paused and looked at my eyes. In a fraction of a moment, I detected that he agreed with me, taking great care not to let the other soldiers see our interaction.

I was told to serve the soldiers when the soup was finished. Somehow I found a way to stumble and spill soup on a German officer. I don't think he liked me very much after that.

Later, I remember walking outside and meeting an officer in charge who began to ask me questions. I told him that I didn't know anything. He sensed my resistance and picked me up by my neck, shook me, and dropped me.

As usual, I had to go to the barn to milk the cows every day. One of the soldiers stood guard at the door. I gave him a dirty look as I walked by. He replied to my muted expression by telling me he didn't want to be here either. He proceeded to tell me that his entire family had been killed in a bombing raid in Berlin. My heart sank into my stomach. I felt so sad for him. He was only 18 years old. I didn't know what to say to him or how to react. Then I remembered there was some cake in the kitchen. I went back into the house, cut a slice, and gave it to him.

At this moment, I realized that what I perceived as the enemy was just another suffering human being. I found my dislike had turned to compassion. This incident had a profound impact on me for the rest of my life. It has helped me look through different eyes and see that we, as human beings, are more alike than different.

The Germans soldiers stayed for another day and arrested everyone in the area who were in the resistance and sent them to concentration camps in Norway. When the Nazi soldiers finally left the farm, they left me behind. Probably because I was too young or perhaps they didn't know what to do with me.

Meanwhile, my parents had heard about the shooting at the farm and went to the German headquarters is Oslo in an effort to find out what had happened to me. They were told that I had been sent to a concentration camp in Germany. Little did they know that I had packed my suitcase, walked for several hours to the nearest train station and was on my way home.

I arrived home in the late evening. My parents were very relieved and happy to see me. How helpless they must have felt. How frightened they must have been.

One year later in May of 1945, the war was officially declared over. It was one of the happiest days of my life. Everybody danced in celebration. The Norwegian underground came out in freedom waving their weapons in victory. I spotted three of my cousins who had served in the underground and we joined in the merriment and great relief of the war's end.

Soon after, the Norwegian government began trials targeted at the Norwegian Nazis. One of the trials involved the man who turned in Christian and Astrid. He was sentenced to prison. Christian and Astrid became Norwegian heroes and were recognized for their sacrifices and the contribution they had made to the war efforts.

One night after I was out celebrating the end of the war, I was walking home when I saw a German vehicle approaching at a high rate of speed. The Nazis now feared retribution from the Norwegians and were frantically trying to get out of the country. They did not know that the king of Norway had declared no retaliation against the Germans and the Norwegian Nazis would have their day in court. As the vehicle got closer, the car hit a bus sign and I had to run out of the way to avoid being hit. I stood and watched them frantically drive away. I was no longer afraid. They could no longer hurt us. We were once again at peace.

—*Ellen Kastler*

The Miracle of Forgiveness

In the summer of 2004, I was extremely busy with a rapidly growing appliance repair business. As a one-man operator, I ran all day, every day, at high speed. Living in the college town of Bellingham, Washington, a high percentage of my business came from property management companies. I did repair work for several firms, and when they would call me, I would go to their offices and pick up work orders and keys for entering the units. I got to know the various property managers and staff, and enjoyed good relationships with them.

One of these companies was very big—they had recently acquired another company and now managed close to 6000 units. They had a good location and a nice office, but their recently hired receptionist was, in my opinion, inept. She constantly gave me the wrong work orders, the wrong address or unit number; there was missing information, incorrect phone numbers, et cetera, but the worst was being given the wrong keys.

After one particularly grueling Friday, when I had been given the wrong keys twice before the right ones were supplied (with a forty-mile round trip to the property each time), I was just about fed up. This woman at the front desk was costing me time and money, but all I could do was bite my tongue, since I didn't want to lose the account. My disdain for her kept increasing, and so did her mistakes. It got to the point where I dreaded going in there and dealing with her.

I had recently begun to read *A Course in Miracles*, and though I had issues with some of the ideas presented, I had a feeling that there was truth and help there, and pressed on with it. On the Monday morning after The Worst Work Day of My Life, I pulled up in front of the aforementioned office in my van, thinking, "I wonder what the screw up will be this time?" Then came the gift. I remembered *A Course in Miracles*' idea of forgiveness, and for some reason, I said out loud, "OK, I'm gonna' go in there as if I've never been there before, like I'm meeting this woman for the first time. It's all brand new. I'm going to see her as my Holy sister." It sounded so strange coming out of my mouth that I laughed!

When I entered the office, the usually disorganized reception area was tidy, and the work orders and keys were delivered to my hands quickly. The whole experienced was breezy, pleasantly efficient, and the formerly somewhat disheveled woman was better looking! Smiles and cheer all around, I was out the door in less than two minutes. When I got to my van I thought, "Wow, that was amazing! What just happened?" The whole experience had changed in the blink of an eye, yet the only thing that I knew for sure was different was my attitude. I realized a miracle had occurred. And the truth that I do make my own reality was made evident to me.

In that moment, my life changed, and has continued evolving in that direction since, though there have certainly been some ups and downs along the way. Everything is alright, Heaven is right here, right now. I am blessed. Thank you, God.

—Ross Osborne

Celebrate Yourself

For fifteen years, I had been rather unhappily married to my second husband. He was very controlling and found fault with everything I did. It seemed that he always managed to find something to complain about; he either cursed at me or criticized me every single day. I had two young daughters from this marriage and two from my first marriage. My self-esteem was very low at the time and I was feeling quite depressed. It was 1987.

One day during this trying time, a friend from church told me about an office manager job at the Ferndale Chamber of Commerce. I met with the woman who was serving as the president and she hired me on the spot. It was a three-hour-a-day position at $5.00 an hour. My youngest daughter started first grade that year, and so I was free to take the job. In addition to doing the bookkeeping and printing the monthly newsletter, I ran the visitor center in Ferndale.

This new job made me feel better about myself, and I met some great people. I became friends with someone on the board of directors. I think he could tell from our conversations that my self-esteem was low, and he was very helpful in suggesting that I join Toastmasters. He also suggested that I read the book *Celebrate Yourself* by Dorothy Corkhill Briggs.

My doctor had encouraged me see to a counselor to help deal with my depression, which I attributed to my upbringing. Most of my issues involved my relationship to my mother. One day when I was in the counselor's office, I discovered a copy of *Celebrate Yourself* and asked to borrow it. The book was enlightening. One of the things that stood out in my mind was the author saying that feelings aren't right or wrong, feelings just are. In other words, one can't control how they feel. So many times when I was growing up I was told, "You shouldn't feel that way." I went around in life with a lot of guilt feelings. The book pointed out to me why I had made my choices regarding husbands; it had to do with how I was raised. As soon as I finished the book, I made the decision to divorce my husband. The thought of getting out of this abusive marriage made me so relieved that when I took my two daughters on a church retreat to Crystal Mountain that weekend, I could have floated up the mountain.

Growing up, I was the oldest girl in a family of six children: three brothers and two sisters. My mother told me one day that she didn't have kids because she wanted them, but because she thought it was her duty. I did most of the housework for my family—I washed the dishes, hung out the clothes to dry, ironed, scrubbed floors, vacuumed, and I also cooked the dinners. My brothers did some of the outside chores, like mowing the lawn. I was doing most of my chores from the time I was about 10 years old. I recall doing something back then that I am almost embarrassed to admit. I was really sick and tired of hanging out the clothes all the time, so one day I took a laundry basket of wet clothes and put them in the garage. I don't know how long it took before it was discovered. In all my growing up years, I never heard a word of praise or received a compliment from my mother, and I didn't receive affection of any kind whatsoever. I certainly never heard the words "I love you."

Many times at Toastmasters meetings, when it was my turn to give a speech, I based it on Briggs's book. Each time, I got the best speech award for the evening, because my speech came from the heart and was unrehearsed. As I recall, I spoke about how unique each one of us is and how we should take pride in our uniqueness. I gave another impromptu speech about the words "I love you," and how it meant different things depending on your tone of voice.

Whenever I spoke to my mother, who lived in Connecticut, I mentioned Brigg's book because it had had such an impact on my life. My mother decided to visit me in Washington while my divorce was pending. When she told my brother Gerry that she was going to visit me, he told her that she was the last person on earth I needed to see, because she always criticized me and found fault with everything that I did. He even told her that she had treated me like I was invisible when I attended my youngest sister's wedding in Connecticut. My mother herself was the one who told me what my brother had said to her when she came for the visit. She asked me if it was true that I felt that way, and I said that I did. She started reading my copy of *Celebrate Yourself* and took it home to Connecticut to finish it. She called me long distance to say that it looked to her as though my ex-husband had taken her place in my life. Since that time our relationship has turned around completely.

In 2001 my stepfather passed away, and my mother moved into my youngest sister's home after paying to have an addition built onto the house to accommodate her. My mother suffered from arthritis and had difficulty getting around. She also gave up driving a car at this time. My sister took care of her needs and fixed her meals for her. My mother paid for the care she received from my sister. After a while, my sister needed a break from caretaking and asked if our mother could stay in my home for a month.

While my mother stayed with me, I did all the things that my sister had been doing for her, including helping her to take baths. This was the first time I really had to take care of her, since she lived in Connecticut. We had an amazing visit. During the course of the visit she said, "I feel like I am getting to know you all over again." I thought to myself, No, you are getting to know me for the first time in your life!

My mother came again the following year and stayed a month and a half. One night before she came for this visit, we were talking about Mt. Baker in a phone conversation and she made a remark that really bothered me, "Speaking of mountains, how is your weight?" When I told her that this comment had upset me, she admitted that it was harsh. I also told her about something that had really upset me when I was around 12 years old, and I received an apology from her for the first time in my life.

My mother passed away on April 9, 2014. By the time of my mother's passing, we had become really close. When I went to her 90th birthday celebration in Connecticut, she was really happy to see me there. She complimented me on the way I had raised my four daughters and even complimented me about how I looked. Our whole relationship had changed and I credit the book *Celebrate Yourself* for that.

—Kathy Chasteen

This Is MY LIFE
and I'm Going to LIVE It

I t took me almost 65 years to find out that life is supposed to be fun! For most of my life I'd been living with negative focus, sadness, unworthiness, and not living up to my true potential because I had such a poor opinion of myself. Depression often took over as I focused on what was wrong in my life: my marriage, my divorce, my religion, my aloneness, my relationships with my children, my financial situation, my lack of career, my failures, lots of failures.

Since the age of 10, I have carried within me the wound of my brother's alleged suicide; this has caused me to be depressed and feel hopeless much of my life. Years later, learning that he did not take his own life didn't help to change the impact his death had on me as a child. My mother shut down and my father disconnected even more from our family. My father was overwhelmed with guilt over my brother's death, and it came out in anger and violence.

As a child I listened to all the happy music and I sang the happy songs; I loved Jiminy Cricket and *Disneyland* on Sunday nights just like other kids. But I had no idea how to be happy. We weren't even allowed to laugh in my family. There was little joy in my life. There was no example of how to choose to be happy. I learned to stay out of my siblings' and father's way.

Later on in life I must have known instinctively that it was important to find joy in my life. There were always moments that gave me joy: listening to birds, appreciating the flowers in my garden, walking, hiking, and biking with friends, playing with my grandchildren. Then I started line dancing and have become quite skilled at it. Now, THAT is fun! I can lose myself for hours! I believe those moments of joy are what saved me from following my brother's example.

We now understand from research that how we feel about ourselves and our life has a powerful impact on our physical health, and feeling happy is the key. I now believe that my depression contributed to the brain tumor that I discovered I had in 2013. The day my tumor became evident, I was taking care of a client and bumped the top of my head so hard it made me sick to my stomach. Five hours later at another client's home, a sudden burst of light in my vision was my wake up call. Thinking it was a stroke I forced myself to see through the bright light to my surroundings. I stood up and focused. When the light subsided I drove home, but along the way I experienced tunnel vision, a classic stroke symptom, though I didn't know that at the time. The sun was in a perfect spot to brighten the road ahead of me, as if the Light was leading me on the right path home.

The next day, after making it through the night without much pain, I drove myself to the emergency room. After a host of tests, a CT scan, and an examination, the young doctor came back into the hospital room where I was lying in bed and said, "Joyce, you have a brain tumor."

The neurologist ordered an MRI to get a clearer picture. After a few visits with him, I began to understand that the tumor was calcified. After two years of MRIs, it was evident that the tumor was not growing. I started thinking that I had dodged the bullet.

Most people would have been shocked into despair and fear at such a prognosis. But I was strangely "chipper," as my son pointed out. Finally, I had the wake up call that life was meant to be satisfying and fun. I finally got it! There's a quote in a picture frame on my windowsill that I just didn't get until then: "This is MY LIFE and I'm going to live it in JOY and GRATITUDE."

Thinking back, there were signs of the tumor along the way. For several years the top of my head had ached, and I intuitively pressed on it at certain pressure points to relieve the pain. Another sign was that my thinking has always been a bit off. I definitely don't think like most people, even as a little girl, and in my teens and twenties I did some really weird things (though maybe that isn't so odd). Now I can blame it on the tumor. Surely my consumption of sugar fed the tumor, as we now know that sugar feeds cancer. I was the chocolate-chip-cookie-pie queen in high school, and while married, I was eating pounds of M & M's every day as a way to medicate my misery. It could have killed me.

Ten years before the diagnosis, I had become acquainted with Norman Vincent Peale and I began to read a lot of books on positive thinking. One day an ad for *The Secret* popped up on my computer screen. I bought the DVD and the book. It was exactly what my soul was longing for. Then, as synchronicity works, I found other sources along the same lines, and soon I was ready to learn more about the Law of Attraction.

This was especially important because I learned that only I

was in control of my thoughts, that it was I who created my life, good or bad. It took awhile for me to really understand this and accept it. I was challenged to consider what I wanted, what I desired in life. I was stumped. I knew what I didn't want; that was easy to come up with. Somehow I had been taught to squelch my desires. Consciously, I didn't want anything. But then I turned those negatives into something positive. I started making lists for different areas in my life, such as spirituality, relationships, and finances. Using what I didn't want, I was able to figure out what I really wanted. That was a powerful time. My creativity was being unleashed and I was allowing myself to dream!

I was so thrilled to have some control that I decided I needed to help other Christians understand and apply the law of attraction. At that time there was nothing on the Internet about the law of attraction aimed at Christians. So I started researching the Bible for verses that matched the meaning of the famous quotations from *The Secret*. I believed that the law of attraction would only resonate with Christians if they heard the words they were familiar with and loved from the Bible. I knew scripture well. After all, I had been a Jehovah's Witness for 20 years (I divorced them in 2000). The enjoyment I received from my research inspired me to write and publish an e-book for Christians about the law of attraction. Eventually, I was ready for the next step of my spiritual education.

When an Abraham-Hicks study group started at Unity Spiritual Center, I jumped on board. The teachings have really given me the power to love and accept myself, to monitor my thoughts, and redirect them. The friends in the group understand each other and respect each other's journey. Abraham-Hicks teachings have put me in touch with myself. We are learning how to realize our potential by bringing ourselves into alignment with who we really are and allowing love and happiness into our lives. You might say I have seen the light! I AM the creator of my life. I create my life by my thoughts.

This new understanding has helped me with some of my elderly clients who have allowed their terrible memories to control their lives and spoil their happiness. I now ask them, "Do you really want to think/talk about this? It is upsetting you," and they catch themselves and stop. I can help distract them, as I've learned to distract myself from thoughts I do not want to continue. My work as a caregiver for people in their last days awakened my gift for understanding the nature of our being. Giving them comfort and encouraging them gave me insight about our deeper spiritual needs. I have found strength and joy in serving others at that time of life to help them have peace of mind knowing that their life did make a difference.

One thing I have learned is that life is meant to be FUN and HAPPY, filled with JOY and LOVE. It is my responsibility to have more fun and see more joy all around me. Just as Jesus said: he came that we might have life and have it more abundantly, that we would have joy and know it more completely. After years of thinking about all of this information and not having any further symptoms, I concluded that a miracle must have already taken place and I didn't even know it. By using pressure points to relieve the pain, drinking kale smoothies, cutting down on sugar, and doing line dancing and practicing the Abraham teachings to find joy in the moment, my life is good. Changing the way I was thinking was the key.

Oh, sure, I sometimes fall back into depression and hopelessness, but then I know I can consciously choose a different emotion, take a nap, work in the garden, take a walk, color a mandala, listen to the birds. This moves me up the scale to an emotion where I can receive all the good that is waiting for me—the delightful experiences, like-minded friends, adventures. The well-being is already there, waiting for me to reach out and embrace it. And so I AM.

Today is a good day. Today is the first day of the rest of my life. Today I will appreciate everything I see and all the people who come into my experience. Today is all there is. Life is good, and I will live it one day at a time. Everything is always working out for me. This is MY LIFE and I am going to LIVE it with JOY and Gratitude. I intend to live up to my name.

—*Joyce Jones*

Chapter 3

Creating Our Reality

Everyday Miracles

How Changing My Way of Thinking about Money Changed My Life

I was self employed in the appliance repair business, and worked very hard to support my family, always keeping a tight grip on expenses. Money was always short; it was a monthly struggle to pay the bills. To save money, I did everything myself. I fixed the cars, built our house—even dug my own well. I also compared my wealth to others, and resented the fact that it sure seemed like I worked a lot harder than they did, but they had more. It's just not fair, I told myself. I seemed to be constantly sick and not very happy. Basically, I was living in a state of constant scarcity. Or rather I should say, Scare City.

Sometimes people wouldn't pay for the work I did, which really ticked me off. I mean, how dare they? It seemed to me that they had tons of money, compared to me. I did a fair bit of work for real estate agents in homes they were selling, in rentals they owned, and in their personal residences as well. At one point, there was a real estate guy that owed me nearly a thousand dollars, most of which was for replacing a water heater in his personal home. I sent repeated statements, wrote letters, called him at his office and home. After all, it was only fair that he should pay for the work I had done, right? Well, after a year or so, he eventually paid me what he owed. But I noticed one day—months after he had paid his account—that whenever he would come to mind I would still feel resentful about how much extra effort I expended to collect what he rightfully owed me. The feeling had become habitual. If I saw his face on a sign, or in an ad, I felt that tightness in my gut and I experienced the resentment again.

What I realized that day was that I was doing it to myself, and I really didn't like the way it felt! The truth was that although it had seemed like there never was enough money, we did have a roof over our heads, the lights were on, we weren't hungry or sick, and there were two cars in the driveway, old ones, but paid for. I would write off (at most) a thousand dollars a year in uncollected accounts. I realized that I was good at the repair business. I was busy all the time, people called me because they needed help, and I really enjoyed solving their problems. I decided then and there that I would concentrate on helping them the best way I could. Because THAT felt good. And let the money take care of itself. I would do the best work I could, always keeping the customer's best interests the top priority. If they paid me, great. If they didn't pay me, well, so what? And, you know what? The money did take care of itself. We always had what we needed. Maybe not everything we wanted, but everything we needed. I made more money after that than I ever had before. Of course, I would still fall into the old pattern at times, but I would usually remember pretty quickly how it felt to truly know that things would be ok. And that really felt so much better than my old habit of worry that I began to repeatedly choose to remember that I was actually do-ing just fine. And from that belief was born a new habit of feeling that my life is abundant.

I also began to give. Before, I would never give away money. Heck, I didn't have money to just give away! But I started giving to charities—just at Christmastime at first. Then to folks begging on the street corners. I wasn't going to church yet, so no «tithing.» One day near Christmas, I saw a woman standing with a sign at the end of the off ramp. It was cold and raining. Pulling out my wallet to hand her a five, I first saw the hundred-dollar bill I had earmarked for Christmas shopping. I said to myself, «I can't give her that!» and kept fishing for the five I was going to give her. Suddenly I knew I MUST give her that Benjamin, as proof to myself that I live in absurd abundance. I folded it up and handed it out the truck window. She took it without looking at it, shoved it into her pocket and scurried back to the corner. As I drove away I grinned, thinking of the surprise she would have later when she pulled it out and saw what it was! Years later I'm still grinning over that event. Talk about bang for your buck! I now know that the way that I can actually feel abundance is to be so confident that there is enough to give some away. I am semi-retired now with a modest fixed income. It's not a lot, but it's enough. Knowing there is enough is what makes it enough. And the cool thing is, I'm not the only one who gets to feel the abundance! If I keep it to myself nobody gets to feel it, not even me! If I give, everybody gets to feel it! I've learned that giving, whether it's money, time, attention, love, work, what have you, is the motive force that brings all these things to me, as well.

I am incredibly blessed. Thank you, God.

—*Ross Osborne*

The Choices We Make

A good friend of mine was unhappily married for most of her life. Her husband of 54 years hadn't been physically abusive, but had been so verbally challenging and contrary that he had totally undermined her self-confidence and sense of self-worth. She could not make an honest statement without having to explain and defend herself. He had so often questioned her choices over the years that she wasn't really sure anymore if she could make a decision on her own. Even a simple "Good morning," would be met with, "It may be good for you, but others aren't as fortunate to feel that way." Or on a clear summer's day with the sun brightly shining he would add, "Yea, but it may not last for long. It'll probably rain by this afternoon." These deflating conversations continually subdued all her desire to even offer an opinion and an air of depression and gloom hung heavily in my friend's life.

"Someday …" she would say, "if I'm lucky he'll just die and I'll finally be free." Tradition had kept her faithful to her marriage vows to "love, honor, and obey," and at first she stayed with him for the sake of the children. Then, when they were older, she was reluctant to leave for fear of their disapproval. And so she became resigned to her fate, and although she secretly prayed to be free, she could never find the courage to move in that direction.

Over the years I learned to accept her decision to remain in the relationship, and listened to her many complaints, but continued to love and support her anyway. Then one morning, as I sat in the waiting room of my dentist's office, I came across a copy of a *New York* magazine with a short poem by Louise Gluck:

> *As I saw it*
> *all my mother's life, my father*
> *held her down, like*
> *lead strapped to her ankles.*
> *She was*
> *buoyant by nature;*
> *she wanted to travel,*
> *go to the theater, go to museums.*
> *What he wanted*
> *was to lie on the couch*
> *with the Times*
> *over his face,*
> *so that death, when it came,*
> *wouldn't seem a significant change. ("New World")*

And this caused me to think about my own mother, who, many years ago, had found herself in a similar situation. She had eloped at the age of 18 to get out of the house, and after a disappointing 38 years of a lonely stifling marriage, finally realized she was trapped with "lead strapped to her ankles." She must have thought, "Nothing is ever going to change and if I stay here, I'm going to die this way … this may well be the end of my life." So Momma made a different decision. At the age of 55 she packed a small suitcase of personal belongings, waited till her husband went to sleep one evening, and walked out into the unknown willing to take a chance on a new life. She went on to live for another 33 years, finally buoyant and free to be her own person. When she died we opened her diary and discovered these words:

"I am on an eternal journey like nothing anyone could ever imagine. It is difficult for me to explain. The worldly and knowledgeable would laugh at an eighty-eight-year-old lady who has visions and dreams such as I. And yet my heart tells me I have found God's Truth, or really, God has found me and made me a part of His Forever Plan of Eternal Participation. The Stradivarius violin lies dormant in its case waiting for the Maestro to play. I am His instrument. He is the music. And I am but the beautiful sounds of the heart created by the Master. I do not play a musical instrument, nor do I sing, dance, paint, draw, write poetry or sculpt. However, I can listen, hear, observe, understand, and appreciate the beauty and passion in the expressions of others. This is my gift as I step out in Faith, carried by God who gives me my words, my thoughts, my actions, and my power. And it is all so wonderful."

When my friend passed away recently, her husband was still lying on his couch with the *Times* over his face. She never did get to do the things she dreamed of. She sadly slipped away with the lead still strapped to her ankles. But Momma lived for another thirty-three years, traveled along many of life's highways, and made a difference in a lot of lives. It's funny the choices we make in life, the paths they put us on, and the lessons we learn. How important it is to unstrap ourselves from the stuff that seems to be weighing us down so that we may experience a "journey like nothing anyone could even imagine." And it's all so wonderful.

—*Jonathan Hall*

I'm Here to Tell the Tale

When I look back at my life in this incarnation, I see how the choices I made and the lessons I needed to learn resulted in emotional pain, guilt, and desperation. One night I felt the most terrible desperation. There was no solution to my muddled thinking, and so I decided to end my life. I had a plan. Just as I was opening the front door to leave, the phone rang. I hesitated for a moment, and went to answer the phone. The call was for my husband, who was not at home. It was a good family friend. At the sound of his voice, I broke down into uncontrollable sobs. This good person and his wife came over immediately. I don't remember what I said to them. But I do remember my father asking me later that night if this was the legacy I wanted to leave my children. That really hurt to hear and it's a good thing his words had such an impact on me.

I remained depressed for a long time. However, I was strong enough to go through the motions of normalcy. I would often go for an evening walk, and my older son would come looking for me. He'd ride his bicycle up and down the streets until he found me, just to know that his mum was alright.

There's an old saying, "Out of everything bad comes something good." Through life's trials, I have learned compassion and forgiveness, not just for myself but for others as well. In being human, we can make wrong choices because it's all we know. My husband and I were married for over fifty years. We had our differences, but he was a good man. We had four beautiful children together, two sons and two daughters. They have taught me so much. I trust they have also learned from me. I believe this is why we are here on Mother Earth, to learn from others.

When I was growing up, the word "love" wasn't used in my family. I knew that my mother loved me. It was expressed in her care for me. But I didn't feel love from my father. He and my mother had a troubled relationship. I became aware of that as I grew older, and carried that wound into my own marriage and family life. Though my husband and I loved our children very much, our "love" was not verbalized to them. It wasn't until my younger daughter Moira, who was fourteen years old at the time, made the suggestion that we, as a family, start saying the word "love" in our communication with each other. Such a thought had never occurred to me! At first, we felt awkward saying, "I love you." One of us would encourage another by saying, "I love you," or simply, "love you." It became part of our experience to end a phone call with the word "love."

Truly love is the most important word in our lives when given from our Spirit within. This was a beautiful lesson for me – to see and feel love. I've learned that my children and my eight grandchildren are gifts loaned by God to my husband and me. My husband is no longer with us. I'm grateful that our family gave him the love and feeling of belonging that he needed. Yes, there will always be upsets and difficulties in family relationships. But Love CAN have deep roots that bind us together, no matter what.

Miracles happen, be they big or small. The Grace of God has deeply touched my life. My Irish auntie once said, "I'm here to tell the tale." And so I have.

—*Maureen Hofstedt*

Ask and You Receive

When my husband Bob and I decided to move back to Bellingham, Washington, after not having lived there for over 30 years, we knew we were about to face a time of big changes. We would be saying goodbye to our Sammamish community and a home and neighborhood we loved, leaving the familiar behind in exchange for the unknown. I had immersed myself in community service in the Seattle area and felt the value of creating small ripples of hope and support in the city. This move would require making all new outreach contacts and basically starting from scratch again, searching for my place within the new community. Unlike Bob, change is not always easy for me, but we both looked forward to what the future had in store for us. That is, until we started house hunting.

We searched the MLS listings daily and soon found we didn't share the same vision for our new home. What one of us thought had potential the other didn't care for at all. Bob was looking at places in the county with five acres and room to raise llamas. I was searching in town so that we could walk or ride a bike to nearby places. I loved older historic architecture; he seemed to lean more towards modern. In the 34 years that we had been together searching for homes, we had never experienced this dilemma. We both were becoming mentally and emotionally drained from the house searching, and realized very quickly that we were not on the same page at all.

Our daughter Chauncey stepped in as the wise sage that she is and suggested that we each make a list of the things that were of utmost importance in a home, then another list of secondary features that would be nice to have but were not essential. We even created a third list of non-essential (but very much desired) features– kind of a fantasy list. To name a few, Chauncey wanted a dance studio, I wanted a craft room, and Bob desired a place on the property for his boat as well as an area for a garden and fruit trees. Few of these desires were easy things to accommodate, but it still was fun to imagine having them. We took our first lists and compared them, only to find that we, in fact, had some common visions. There was hope after all! We wrote those items down on a new list, and then talked about our secondary lists and found more shared views, adding them to our new list as well. When we got to the fantasy list, we refused to toss it and decided we would keep these wishes on the back burner of desire.

Once we had clear intention of what we wanted, the Universe moved quickly. Within two weeks we found a house that had everything that we wanted in the price range we could afford. Amazingly, not only did the house meet our entire list of primary and secondary needs, but it provided everything that we had listed on our fantasy list—including the dance studio! At that moment we began calling it our "miracle home" because it truly was a miracle. We love our home, don't miss not owning llamas, and feel the blessing of Bellingham being our community. We are grateful.

—Mary Trask

The Way Life Is Supposed to Be

In the first year of my life (1941–42), my family lived in a historic house in Portland, Oregon. I like to think that's how my interest in old houses and antiques got started. It was an exceptional turn-of-the-century Victorian house, but it was in terrible condition when my dad found it. No one was living in the house and it had been vandalized. My dad didn't like to see this property mistreated. So he found the owner and offered to fix it up. Dad was a chiropractor, but he worked on houses on the side. Our family moved in and rented the place for just $10 a month.

As I grew up, my dad took me along on his jobs and taught me how to do carpentry and electrical wiring. The electrical side of things really interested me. My best friend Wayne Linschied and I helped to start the Science Club at our high school. We had Army Surplus modified ham radios and transmitters in our cars and homes, and we served Civil Defense with our radios. After high school, I got an A.S. in Electronics and started working as a service technician in Salem, Oregon.

On one of my first jobs I met a technician who owned 20 houses. I was impressed with that and decided to start buying and fixing up houses myself. I bought my first house on a service call. The owner of the property was discouraged with renting to tenants. He said he'd sell the place for $5000 if someone would take it off his hands. So I found a friend to help me buy it and ended up owning the place myself.

When I married my second wife, Gloria, I had just bought and sold three houses. By this time, I had a lot of work experience: electronic service, antenna installation, technical writing, city bus driver. I also had taught college math and electronics theory. But I didn't have the wisdom to be a father to my stepchildren—three boys and two girls. A friend recommended for us to go to the Science of Mind Church. He thought maybe this church would be able to help us, because the older kids were not adjusting and I wasn't either. We met the Camerons, a 70-year-old man and his wife, who were ministers personally trained by Ernest Holmes, and we signed up for their first-year practitioner course. Coming to this church was a great choice for us, as it helped our oldest boy to turn himself around.

For about a year, Gloria and I had been saying affirmations to stay positive and we always helped to correct each other's thinking. Positive thinking changed our whole outlook. We decided to take our family on a camping trip to Vancouver during my summer vacation. On our way back to Oregon we stayed overnight in Bellingham, Washington. We loved the town so much that I put in an application for employment at a service center. Three weeks later, they called and said to come to work. One month later, we were on our way to hunt for a house in Bellingham.

On the second day, we drove out to Squalicum Lake Road and pulled into a driveway where an older man was trying to put ignition points in his tractor. I said, "Can I help you with that?" and proceeded to install the point condenser. I asked him if there were any houses for sale in the area. He said that his neighbors were moving in a month, so we went over to see them. They had a three-bedroom house on 10 acres with a 1930s barn and a root cellar. It was perfect for us. So we signed a contract with a $5000 deposit. The owners let us stay in their lake cabin until they moved out. Was this miraculous? This kind of thing was normal for us.

My new job at the service center went well that first year. I became lead technician and completely furnished the service shop with top-of-the-line equipment, and then I was laid off. With six kids (Gloria and I added a baby girl to our family), no job, and house payments, my wife started a consignment shop and I started a TV service company. We spent the next few months searching for anything saleable for Gloria's shop. I went to every service company in Bellingham and offered to repair anything for $25.00. During that time, we helped start a Religious Science study group at the Leopold Hotel.

A year later, Gloria and I moved our family into a historic home on Walnut Street. One morning, a man knocked on our front door and handed me a bag of silver dollars to save for him while he looked for a job. He soon moved in with us and helped me double the size of our home. During that time, I took ownership of an electronics division with a partner. We made the sales record from Seattle west to the Canadian border. The following year, I traded the store to my partner for the latest electronic equipment for our home. My wife opened Gloria's Web on James Street. Another year, another shop—Fountain Antiques. Then we started Olden Oak Antiques. We purchased antiques from shops in Vancouver and the Canadians would bring trucks to buy from us. We had a large inventory by then, so in 1976 we purchased a 12,000 sq. ft. warehouse.

In 1978, Wardner's Castle at 1103 15th Street appeared on the front page of the *Bellingham Herald* stating: *Historic 12,000 sq. ft. castle for sale.* It was designed by the architect Kirtland Cutter. My wife Gloria had been carrying a picture of this house in her purse since we first drove through Bellingham. On the picture, she had written, "Our house some day." We went through the castle quickly, because it was 5:00 in the evening. The realtor already had two offers. Without even going upstairs to look, we said we'd take it. This was the most expensive house that had ever been listed in Bellingham. I had no steady job, but we promised a $25,000 down payment in 30 days. We borrowed money, traded a percentage of our antique warehouse for a condo in Fairhaven, and sold the Walnut Street house, turning down the first good offer, and holding out for a cash offer, which happened that week. We had more than enough for the sale. The first two offers the owner got on the castle fell through, and we were in.

Gloria and I took a lot of risks, not knowing whether things would work or how we would afford it. But we didn't worry. We just expected that everything we needed would come along. That's how we found the castle. We never watched to see if it had come up for sale.

This was the twelfth house I had purchased. We were having so much fun by now, we almost forgot we were dealing and trading and buying houses and antiques seven days a week, and restoring all of this besides. We spent the next twenty years restoring the castle and its 23 rooms while living there, and traveled to Europe, Southeast Asia, Mexico, Central America, and all over the U.S. to buy antiques. We put Wardner's Castle on the National Register. In the end, I received an achievement award from Mayor Douglas for the restoration work on the castle.

In 2000, we sold the castle to an arts and antiques dealer. That was a year of big change for us. We discovered that my wife Gloria had lung cancer. We moved into the 950 sq. ft. waterfront cabin that we had been renting to the spiritual teacher and mystic Elizabeth Burrows. We sold 95% of our collections and purchased two commercial buildings in Ferndale. My wife designed the Spanish remodel in the smaller building and I started a clock shop.

We had owned these buildings in Ferndale for two years when we decided to sell them. They sold on the same day we listed them. Gloria wanted me to establish another clock shop, so we rented a space along with 12 other shops in Lynden. My wife helped paint and decorate. She was getting radiation treatments, which halted tumor growth, but it didn't stop the cancer from spreading to other areas. So in 2007, we went to Mexico for some experimental treatments. Sadly, the treatments at the clinic were not successful. Gloria progressively became weaker and in November of that year, she passed peacefully.

Needless to say, the loss of Gloria in my life after 38 years of marriage was hard to bear. But I continued to run the clock shop in Lynden that year and decided to sign another one-year lease. The insurance company came into the shop and asked me to reinstate my policy for a $20 fee and cancel it later. Three days later, the building was gutted by fire and I collected the insurance. That was fortunate, but the loss of so many beautiful antique timepieces under my care was extremely stressful.

Soon after the fire, I received a card from our friend Eugenia, who had once rented the cabin from Gloria and me. The message said, "Now that the barn is gone, you can see the moon." Eugenia brought new light into my life. I hesitated pursuing her because of my fragile state of mind, but I had a feeling we would soon be together. Two years later, we exchanged our vows.

There's no such thing as a miracle. That's just the way life's supposed to be.

—*Larry Harriman*

Chapter 4

Healing Is Believing

Everyday Miracles

Going Back to the Basics

During the first two weeks of February 2016, I experienced the worst health of the past 28 years of my life. Initially I thought it was food poisoning, brought on by the longneck razor clam soup I had made and consumed the previous day. Sweats ... Lord were there sweats! Sweat drenched my tee shirt and turned my pillow into a sponge. Then the chills took over. I am talking chills down to the bone. Even after climbing under the covers with all my clothes on and setting my electric blanket on the highest temperature, my teeth were still chattering. It had been almost three decades since I experienced sickness that would go on like this for days and days.

I watched my behavior as the 4th, 5th, and 6th day came and went without any noticeable improvement. I tried to become one with the illness. I didn't beat myself up for not going to work or for shirking my household responsibilities. I just allowed myself to read, sleep, and eat. I embraced the illness that had appeared in my life and was determined to just let it run its course. Finally ... on the 10th day, I felt strong enough to go outside and do a little yard work. Wow, that illness was ugly! It took a total of two weeks before I felt stable, balanced, and confident enough to go back to work. Focus is important when you're working eight feet in the air, supported by home-built scaffold, standing on an aluminum plank 14-inches wide by 26-feet long, with no handrail. I was grateful to be well enough to do my job again, and I vowed to practice the wisdom I had learned about thirty years ago.

It was the second week of January 1988 when, as a newly married husband, my wife and I attended our first session with a study group on *A Course In Miracles*. From that study, soon followed the teachings of Charles and Myrtle Fillmore, founders of the Unity movement. I read with fascination about the five basic Unity principles. The principles seemed so easy, and they made sense. It seemed believable that I could create whatever I wanted or desired by using affirmations and denials.

What a blessing, what a freedom I had been introduced to with this new teaching. There is no room for victims when you realize that you are truly the creator of your life. I start by saying what it is that I am creating; next I affirm it; then I live it, moving boldly forward without doubt, resistance, or hesitation. For example, I would say: "My body is enjoying perfect health, I affirm my body is at peace, and I am enjoying that peace with the abundance of perfect health." I then truly know it is done and complete, and live it with all my heart and soul.

I was captivated by Myrtle Fillmore's account of healing herself from the death sentence of tuberculosis. Her mantra—to bless every single cell in her body and affirm that she was a child of God and did not inherit sickness or disease—became mine. I would recite this phrase over and over to myself until I believed it. Then I lived it. The results were next to phenomenal.

Up until those weeks in February 2016, I had experienced less than a handful of sick days in 28 years. I know that was because I affirmed my well being by using Myrtle Fillmore's guidance. Looking back on those ten days of illness, I realize that I had been taking my health for granted. I wasn't creating the perfect health I was desirous of. I was no longer re-affirming that I was the creator that I truly am: "I am a child of God and I do not create sickness or disease." I am going back to the basics.

—*Russell A. Eiriksson*

The Wise Doctor

Growing up as a child, I believed that I was sickly because that is what my mother always told me. Apparently, I was born with whooping cough, which led to pneumonia, and that had weakened my lungs. When I was nine years old, I became so weak that I was almost disabled. My parents were members of the Apostolic Faith and my mother was a devout believer. I remember her getting down on her knees and saying prayers for me every day. Her praying embarrassed me so much that I stopped bringing kids home to play. My parents used to take me to church with them every Sunday until I got too sick to leave the house. It got to the point where my bodily functions were starting to fail, and I was bedridden. My father, who was a chiropractor, was knowledgeable about the body and natural medicine and dietary health. But my good diet hadn't helped me any more than my mother's prayers.

One day, without my mother's or my consent, my father decided to take me to Doernbecher Children's Hospital in Portland, Oregon, to have the doctors examine me. My mother angrily resisted my dad's decision and I didn't want to leave home, so we both struggled against him. To get me out of the house and carry me to the car, my dad had to ask a neighbor to help him. It was a long drive to Portland, about sixty miles away from our home.

My father left me at the hospital after the doctors finished examining me. They didn't know what was wrong with me, and probably thought it was all in my head. They said that I needed to stay there for three weeks to see how I would respond to some new medicine and physical therapy. They gave me some kind of powder dissolved in water. I didn't mind that because I was used to taking medicine. The first thing they do at the hospital is make you walk. I had to get up and do exercise every morning. Soon I was strong enough to sit in a wheel chair.

My parents lived too far away to come and visit me at the hospital during my stay. I felt scared and I badly wanted to go home. It was a totally new and unfamiliar place and I didn't know anyone there. Because my mother was overly protective, I had trust issues. I remember seeing the x-rays on the wall of the examining room. The insides were in the wrong places. In one of them the heart was on the right side, and the organs were twisted. I worried that maybe that was my own x-ray. But I didn't have any medical issues that showed up on an x-ray. The doctor said that I was way too aware of physical problems for someone my age. I saw other kids my age at the hospital with far more serious problems than I had, and I noticed that they were still happy. That was a big lesson for me.

When the three weeks had finally passed, my parents came to take me home. The doctor asked me if I was ready to leave. By that time, I was having such a good time with the other kids at the hospital that I didn't want to go home, so my parents let me stay another week. Some of us kids liked to climb out through the window and play on the roof, or we'd have wheelchair races down the hall. People would come in and teach us leather crafts and fly tying. I was having a good time. I felt strong and I no longer needed the wheelchair. So I was fully cured and ready to leave the hospital after one month.

When my parents came to take me back home, the doctors told me I didn't need to take the medicine anymore. They said it was a placebo—it didn't do anything. I was afraid to stop taking that medicine, because I thought it was the only reason I had gotten well. It was then that I realized I had cured myself by what I thought and believed. I knew that my mother loved me, but she had believed I was a sick child and so I stayed sick, believing that to be the truth. The truth is that whatever you choose to believe, if you believe it long enough, you will accept it as true.

—*Larry Harriman*

My Path to Wholeness

There are times in life when illness actually results in a positive life transformation, with knowledge gained that was unknown before. It can give us a new awareness of possibilities, and open us to other methods of healing. After experiencing a plethora of illnesses growing up, everything came to a turning point at age 22 when the doctors wanted to do exploratory surgery. This was certainly not an option for me. Some good friends in Fort Collins, Colorado, suggested seeing a naturopathic doctor in their town. My dad agreed to fly me there, as we were curious about how he could help me.

To my amazement, after one week of taking the nutritional supplements the doctor had prescribed, and adjusting my food intake, I felt better than I had in years. From that point forward, I began my journey of studying everything possible to learn more about natural and alternative medicine modalities. My health continued to improve and my knowledge increased, resulting in being able to teach classes on herbal medicine, homeopathy, iridology, and how our food is our medicine.

After continuing to study and apply my newfound knowledge, I became fully aware that my physical condition was directly related to my emotional, mental, and spiritual body being out of balance. My physical body had been reacting in unhealthy ways for many years to what my emotional, mental, and spiritual body felt but did not know how to express. Learning how the mind and body are connected finally gave me the insight to be open to other modalities of healing. My feelings were Energy-in-Motion (E-motion), which felt like a mess at the time.

By now I was approaching age 39 and wanted to know how to BE the person I felt I was inside. There was a naturopathic doctor in Spokane, where I lived at the time, who was highly recommended, so I called his office for an appointment. Since he was out of town, I made an appointment with his physician's assistant. This was okay, since I was just going in for a physical. As it turned out, this assistant was the person I was destined to connect with for my next step to wellness. After discussing my health history and completing the exam, she shared with me that she was facilitating a workshop series, which turned out to be "just what the doctor ordered." I was intrigued and eager to learn about this new way of healing. This experience was a huge step toward a renewed life of learning, exploring, and listening to Spirit. From this point forward, I attracted just the right teacher at just the right time for what was next for me to learn and experience.

Living each day with an attitude of gratitude while also living a life of learning takes continual focus. It means never giving up being attracted to new modalities and accepting that the right teacher will show up at the right time. "When the student is ready the teacher appears." Every. Single. Time.

—RoseMarie Longmire

Healing Power of Love

As I look back over my life, I am keenly aware at 65 that there have been many miracles and serendipitous events in my life, for which I am eternally grateful. As Jesus says in *A Course in Miracles*, "There is no order of difficulty in miracles."

The most life-changing experience was my healing of Hepatitis C. In early 1993 as a result of donating plasma, I was sent a letter from the blood bank that I could no longer donate because my blood tested positive for Hepatitis C. I was retested a couple of times and the initial test results were true. I had been feeling very fatigued for a while, but felt it was due to stress. I had to leave my job because of the fatigue. Over the years through the power of grace, I managed to live life, enjoyed life, and accepted my limitations. I was blessed with an amazingly supportive husband and son. During this time we had no medical insurance, so I was unable to have any treatment. However, while initially the physicians were saying I would need a liver transplant, the virus never progressed to cause any substantial damage to my liver.

In 2000 my mother-in-law passed away and left us with a substantial inheritance. Again, grace blessed us. Now I had the funds to seek treatment. Much to the amazement of the liver specialist, my liver was healthy; however, he cautioned that at any moment the virus could activate and I would be in trouble.

In 2003 I started experiencing symptoms again of extreme fatigue, insomnia, and abdominal tenderness. My liver enzymes were going up and the physicians wanted to start me on some very toxic medications. I prayed and meditated and felt that there was no need to panic, so I declined any treatment.

On September 18, 2004, my dearest love, Paul, died suddenly of cardiomyopathy. We had had 33 glorious years together and now I had to adjust to life without him. Again, my faith sustained me, along with the support of my devoted son, family, and friends.

In August of 2005, I was at a low point, feeling sick and sorry for myself. I sat down to meditate, sobbing. I felt a tap on my shoulder, yet no one was there. I heard a voice ask me, "Why are you suffering my child?"

"Because I am supposed to," I responded.

"Do you really believe the Father wants his child to suffer?"

"NO," I said.

"That is the answer I wanted to hear." And then he said, "Close your eyes and feel the love that you are, and the love that embraces you, breathes you, and beats your heart ... YOU ARE HEALED."

I fell asleep and when I awoke ten hours had passed. From that moment on, I have never been ill or sick. I had my naturopath order a blood test for hepatitis C. The results were NEGATIVE—not a trace of virus.

Since then, I have been blessed with another wonderful loving relationship. My heart is overflowing with deep gratitude and peace. Where I am LOVE IS AND ALL IS WELL.

—Helga DeLiban

Chapter 5

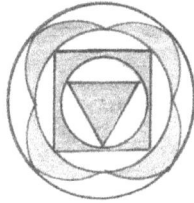

Miracles of Healing

Everyday Miracles

The "New" Bob

August first of 1999 was a comfortably warm day in Phoenix. The blistering heat of July had pretty much moved on and I was enjoying working with my roses in the back yard when the phone rang. My wife Stephanie brought the phone out to me and said, "It's Emily."

As soon as I finished saying hello to our daughter, Emily blurted out in a highly excited voice: "Dad, Uncle Bob fell off a ladder and they don't thinks he's going to survive!" My knee-jerk reaction was, "Emily, don't be ridiculous, people don't die from falling off a ladder."

My brother Bob was at a residential lot with his wife Jan, and my oldest brother's widow, Ruth. Bob and Jan were planning on building there and he was cleaning out some brush and pruning trees. After Jan and Ruth headed home to start dinner, Bob climbed to the top of his twelve-foot ladder to prune one last tree.

For some reason that we will never know, he came "flying" out of the top of the tree. For another reason we will never know, my brother was unable to make any attempt to protect himself before hitting the ground. He landed in the rocks below, taking the direct hit on the right side of his forehead and face. Fortunately, a neighbor out dumping his garbage saw it happen.

The neighbor immediately called 911. Miraculously, there was a fire station very near by, and the paramedics were on the scene in less than three minutes. They later reported that they did not think Bob would be alive by the time they reached the hospital.

After Jan and Ruth had been alerted and arrived at the hospital, they were told there was little chance Bob would survive through the night and relatives should be notified. That's when I got the call from Emily.

Harborview Medical Center is recognized as one of the foremost trauma and burn centers in the country. Patients from all over the world are flown there for treatment of the most critical injuries. Miraculously, my brother did survive the night. I arrived in Seattle the next day and was shortly at Harborview. Bob's wife, Jan, our sister-in-law Ruth, and several of her kids (my nephews) met me at the waiting area on the ICU floor.

I asked to see my brother and the nurse gave permission. My nephew Steve (then in his twenties) walked back to the room with me. On the way he said, "Uncle Jon, you're not going to recognize Uncle Bob so be prepared."

I guess my first thought was, "My God, he looks like a Martian." His badly bruised head was the size of a basketball, had a steel rod sticking out of the top, and his eyes were purple lumps the size of golf balls. I took his hand and mumbled something I don't remember. I do remember him squeezing my hand firmly.

Getting information from any of the doctors was next to impossible, and especially frustrating. They were willing to share that the next three days were critical and IF Bob survived he would not be the same person as before the accident. They could not tell us what deficiencies he would have, but guaranteed us that there would be some number of them.

That afternoon Jim Jansen, president of his family-owned Lynden Company, came to the hospital. Jim is one of most intelligent and totally incredible people I have ever met. Jim hired my brother away from another company. Bob started and managed a new company for a number of years in Alaska, and was now a senior manager at the Lynden Company headquarters in Seattle, Washington.

I knew Jim, too. I had been invited on company fishing trips in Western Alaska. We took Alaska Airlines from Anchorage to King Salmon in southwest Alaska. From there Jim took us in his floatplane further out to the fish camp.

After our mother died, Jim flew out of Anchorage to the Chugach Mountains to disperse the ashes of my mother, brother, and father in the mountains. A couple of years later when our dad died, Jim flew Bob and I to the same spot to leave his ashes there, too.

Jim told Jan to not worry about anything other than her husband's recovery. He shared the comforting news that he had assigned a lady at the office to monitor and manage every detail of the medical expenses, take care of payments, and that my brother would stay on the payroll until he was able to return to work.

Jim also advised us: "Don't pay attention to the doctors because they don't know what's going to happen." Jim has a son that has epilepsy and he has spent plenty of time studying the brain (remember, I told you how intelligent he is). He explained that the doctors are not incompetent but that the human brain is SO complex there is no way, at this time, to know what it is capable of doing.

Well, Bob did survive those next three days, but was still

critical. During that time Jan and I attended several "classes" that were intended to prepare us for dealing with the "new" Bob and his deficiencies, assuming he survived.

During this time I was unable to meet the doctor who had treated Bob the night he arrived at the ER. This would be the one who had removed a piece of his skull to relieve the swelling in the brain. When I asked for his assessment, he started doing the "doctor dance" with a lot of "No way to tell" responses. Quickly running out of patience I said, in a rather demanding voice, "You were there! You removed his skull! You SAW his brain! I want to know what you SAW!"

After a short period of silence: "Your brother received serious damage to 75% of the right hemisphere of his brain. There is no way to know the extent of his deficiencies, IF he survives." I thanked him and left the room. At least we now have some facts, and I can deal with facts.

I could write a novel to relate the events that miraculously unfolded from that day forward. The healing process that took place over the following days, weeks, and months would simply be a testament to the strength and dedication of my brother's wife Jan, the power of faith and prayer, and the resilience and unending optimism of the human spirit.

With his wife at his side, Bob was moved from Harborview, first to Swedish Hospital (more about healing and less about trauma), and then to a rehabilitation center, and eventually home, with continued outpatient rehab.

A bit later, Jim Jansen and the rest of the miraculous group at Lynden Company welcomed Bob back to work for a couple hours a day. And then he was back for four hours a day, and on

August 1, 2000 (exactly one year after the accident) he returned to work full time.

Oh, by the way, except for decreased hearing in his right ear, Bob has no deficiencies as a result of the accident. Did his right hemisphere repair itself? Did his left hemisphere "rewire" itself and take over the duties of the damaged right hemisphere? Who knows? Who cares? Maybe Jim Jansen is even more intelligent than I thought.

Bob retired from Lynden Company last year and they hired one person, and later added a second person to replace him. I guess he did quite a job for a guy with half a brain.

He and Jan have been touring around the "Lower 48" in their Motor Coach since the retirement. They have been across the country to the mid-west, down to Florida, and back across the southwest to California visiting old friends and meeting new ones, as they think about where they might want to stay summers and winters.

We talk a couple of times a week. Mostly about nothing, just to stay connected. As I'm writing this, they're on their way from San Diego to Palm Springs for a month or so. They will be back in Washington in early summer for annual visits with their relatives (and doctors). They'll be coming to Bellingham in July to visit their niece Emily, her husband, and the three grandkids. They are pretty excited about being at our daughter Megan's wedding while they're here, too.

After that? They will be on their way again … just enjoying the "Miracle of Life."

—Jon Strong

Angels Watching Over Me

I don't believe that it's possible to explain the miraculous happenings in our lives as mere coincidences. I believe that Angels are here with us in this world. One day, when I was about four years old, my mother told me I could play outside with my young friend Jimmy. I was told to stay close to home, and apparently, I did not listen. I was run over by a car!

The first thing I can remember is lying on the ground underneath a big black car looking up at the profile of a woman. She was dressed in black and wore a large black hat. I was sure she was a witch. The woman was sitting in the driver's seat. She must have been stunned by what had happened. I remember that my legs were underneath the car, touching neither the front nor the rear tires. What a miracle that I was not crushed! The car wheels never touched me at all. The other astonishing thing is that this accident happened in front of the local drugstore. The druggist knew my family well. I remember him picking me up and carrying me to my mother's door. My young friend Jimmy, who was so upset at seeing me in such a state, ran home feeling sick.

The angels visited me again in my early childhood. When I was five years old I had peritonitis. It began with a tummy ache and the pain increased in severity. My mother was concerned about me and called our family doctor for advice. Oddly enough, the doctor said it was just a stomachache and that it would soon go away. But my mother persisted in calling the doctor for advice until he finally agreed to send a blood specialist to our home. A sample was taken and it was determined that my pain was more serious than a stomachache. I was rushed to the hospital to have my appendix removed.

Though I don't remember saying it, my mother later told me that before the operation, I had said to the doctors and nurses, "Please tell me a ghost story." Maybe I was just trying to delay the inevitable. I remember the green mask filled with ether coming down over my face. It was terrifying! My parents were sitting outside the door of the operating room, and they could hear me screaming. My mother told me that I had called to her, saying that the Angels were coming. My mother, being Irish and stubborn, assured me that the Angels were not coming. I am quite sure that a mother who loves her child would not have to be Irish to say this! She would do everything in her power to keep her child on the earth. Upon reflection, I am sure that the Angels did come to save me. The poison had spread throughout my body. At that time, sulfa drugs were used to treat peritonitis, as penicillin was not yet available. It was truly a miracle that I survived. So many who suffered from peritonitis did not.

My healing process, both in the hospital and at home, took a long time. I spent six long months in the hospital before I could go home. I remember the day my Aunt Lal and Mum came into my hospital room to tell me I could come home. It was Easter Sunday. There was a big chocolate bunny sitting on my table, and I was coloring a picture when they walked in the door.

After I returned home, I remember having to wear a surgical corset around my waist with big rubber binders around my legs for months afterwards, partly because I dragged my left leg. My parents never gave up on me. They called in every possible specialist to take care of me. They even enrolled me in tap dancing lessons, though all I could do was shuffle. I have a fond memory of my mother patiently wrapping my limp hair in rag curlers to bring back the curl. I finally did recover enough to return to school. By then I was 7 years old. Unfortunately, to pay the medical bills, we had to sell our house and move into an apartment hotel. Never did I hear a word of complaint from either of my parents. I was so blessed. Thank you, God.

—*Maureen Hofstedt*

The Miracle Baby

W hen I was a little girl, my always mother told me that I was a miracle. During my gestation, she had been ill with a syndrome called preeclampsia. In December of 1961, I was unexpectedly delivered by cesarean section, as my mother had had a seizure and was fighting for her own life. The sisters of Holy Trinity Community Hospital in Clarkston, Washington, gently placed all 3 pounds of me on a warming bed with a plastic dome over the top, and prayed throughout the night. I was approximately 33 weeks old.

My mother and I were placed side by side in the intensive care unit. The MD filled out our death certificates and instructed the sisters to call and let him know the time of death for one or the other of us, so he could sign off. He left the number of the Elks Club where he could be reached and returned to dinner. My mother's brother attempted to contact my father, who was a sheriff, but he could not be reached at that hour.

My uncle ignored the nursing staff and the sisters at the ICU, and came in and sat down between my mother and me. He made it his mission to rub our sternums, at any given time, if he felt we had stopped breathing; or he would blow on our faces if we turned a paler shade of white. He mercilessly bullied the sisters for warm blankets, more prayers, or company for us during his vigil, all the while demanding coffee and updates from the staff. Sixteen weeks, one hemorrhage, and one code blue later (and now single), my mother left the hospital with me to join my sisters and our grandparents at their home.

I came into life with all kinds of health issues, but the strength and courage of my mother was in me, too. As I grew into adulthood, I found out that I am my mother's daughter. Like her, I would face big challenges with getting pregnant and keeping pregnancies. I have one adopted child and two other children who were conceived through the science of IVF and the Great Spirit. My younger two are eight years apart. They were willed into existence by thousands of dollars of debt, manifested through desire and fierce love, with the knowledge that I would bring something amazing into this world.

The youngest child was the biggest miracle of all. Eric Hayden. I knew the name before the child, as I had felt his presence in me and he gifted me with it in 1998. It was a bittersweet pregnancy, wracked with multiple health complications and preterm delivery. My obstetrician would later joke that I was not to darken her door ever again, and that of all her clients, I was the only person who could carry a pregnancy to 35 weeks and deal with four threatening illnesses: PUPP 's, preeclampsia, gestational diabetes, and incompetent cervix. My womb was hostile. My heart and Eric's indomitable will were not. We bled, seized, starved, and damn near stroked out, but lived and loved each other into existence.

December 4, 1998. That day is forever engraved in our psyche. I felt unusual, kind of spacey and tired, and had not felt Eric move for what seemed like a long while. I called the hospital to go in and have a fetal well-being strip done. Ten hours and two procedures later, with blood found in the amniotic fluid, I was told it was imperative that my son be born NOW. Eric arrived after only 45 minutes of labor, from start to finish. Bawling hysterically, as he placidly lay on my chest, we fell in love. Fifteen minutes later he was transported out of my arms and into the natal intensive care unit. Sometime during the previous 24 hours, he had sustained a neonatal stroke and was paralyzed on the right side of his body with brain trauma. It took a year of challenging, threatening, and negotiating with the insurance company for my husband and I to see the damage revealed on a CT scan by a neurologist. We were told that his future was uncertain and that only Eric and time would tell, but not to hope for much, due to the location and size of the scarring on his brain.

Through guts, determination, desire, and love—megawatts of love—plus family support, Eric has surpassed, blown away, and tossed away all poor expectations of him. He has endeared all who have encountered his beautiful spirit. Generous, forgiving, funny, loving, and loyal, he has 3007 stitches, 11 broken bones, 3 grafts, and an unlimited supply of patience and goofiness, with an above average intelligence that will carry him to great things. I would like to think that I somehow resuscitated him inside of me, but I know this is not true. Great Spirit, in its infinite love, wanted to suffer, live, experience, and glorify the human existence of soul in Eric. Our creator is in for a rousing crazy ride and is laughing all the way, while I stand by and smile like only a mother can.

—*Christa Armstrong*

Memories from a Hamburg Townhouse

Soon after Christmas of 1942, I became very sick. I had a high fever and extreme difficulty breathing. I was seven years old at the time. Our pediatrician Dr. Deckwitz diagnosed me with diphtheria and scarlet fever. He therefore recommended immediate transfer to the Eppendorf Hospital near Hamburg. Mom refused to let me out of the house because the Allies had repeatedly bombed the hospital, and many people in the building had been injured or killed. The Nazis were notorious for abusing the Red Cross sign, and it no longer served as a protection for hospitals. So a surgeon was notified to come to our home to perform an emergency operation.

I was moved out of the room I shared with my little sister to my older brother Carli's room in the East suite on the third floor, as Carli had returned to boarding school forty miles south of the city. His room looked very different. Gone were the bookcases with all the cowboy and Indian stories and science fiction books. His beloved tinker toy contraptions had been put away. The movie posters were still on the walls but the carpet was gone. My bed was positioned in the middle of the room, where I lay under a feather bed with a feeding tube in my arm. A surgeon arrived at the house with two assistants: an anesthesiologist and a surgical nurse. Aunt Mischa, as former obstetric nurse, also assisted.

When I woke up, I was able to breathe through a tube inserted in my neck. It was uncomfortable, but I was given pain medication and did not complain. Dr. Deckwitz injected me with a diphtheria vaccine he had developed and wanted to test. It worked in a short while and the other children in my family were also vaccinated. Pretty soon I could breathe without the use of a tube in my throat. The scarlet fever persisted, however, and I had to stay in bed until early February. During those weeks, I lay in that room on the third floor under the feather bed hallucinating. The windows in my room were wide open and the noise from the outside was terrifying. Sirens were sounding, anti-aircraft guns shooting, bombs detonating, fire engines blaring ... The family cook prepared bone broth and light foods for me at the instruction of my mother and slowly I began to recover.

Finally, in the beginning of February, the fever was gone. Although I was still weak, Mom wanted us to leave Hamburg immediately and she drove us with Aunt Mischa to a sanatorium in Bafd Salzungenm in the mountains of Thuringia in central Germany, where I recuperated. She stayed for a few days of rest, then drove back home. The operation that saved my life left me with a scar on my throat and another problem: a damaged thyroid gland that left me struggling for energy all of my life.

On January 27,1943, while I was still sick in the room on the third floor, Hamburg experienced one of most devastating daytime air raids of the war. An attack with incendiary bombs, targeting the St. Nikolai parish area just east of downtown, destroyed block after block, mile after mile of apartment houses where the port workers lived. Only the tower of the church remains standing in that neighborhood as a memorial to those who died in the fires.

Three years later, when the war was over, our family drove in silence through St. Nikolai on the way to the 75th anniversary of the C. Friese Company. We saw only rubble and ruins, no occupied houses until we reached the northeast suburb of Wandsbek where my family's factory was located. That building had burnt several times during the war. What was once an imposing four-story, early 20th century building had been reduced to a modern two-story building.

Not until recently, when I researched the bombing of Hamburg during the Second World War, did I realize that my whole family was in the city when the firebombing had occurred. (Complete Royal Air Force (RAF) records of every raid on Hamburg are posted on Wikipedia.)

Many miracles happened that winter. First miracle: Our family pediatrician Dr. Deckwitz had created the diphtheria vaccine that worked its magic. Second miracle: my mother knew about the proper nourishment for a very sick child (bone broth). Third miracle: I was strong enough to make it through the fevers. Fourth miracle: The Allied planes dropped all their bombs on one targeted area and got away as fast as they could because the flames shot up sky high threatening the airplanes themselves. Usually attacking planes would drop the rest of their load anywhere on their way back to England, but this time they had no bombs left and simply fled. Consequently, many neighborhoods, including ours, were spared during that bombing raid of January 1943.

Now I also understand why my mother took us out of the city as soon as she could. I did not remember any of these traumatic events until 1982, when I was having bodywork done at the

Stress Management Center in Baltimore, Maryland. As the body worker was massaging my shoulder I suddenly screamed in pain. He asked, " What are you seeing?"

I said: "I see myself on the top floor of our house in Hamburg. I am alone in the middle of the room under a feather bed. I am hot with fever. The windows are open. The noise outside is frightening; I can hear the sound of fire engines and bombs exploding, and the anti-aircraft guns shooting."

He said, "This memory is stuck in your cells. With your permission I will work on releasing it. Are you willing to go through that with me?"

"Yes, that is why I am here," I said.

It took many more sessions and hard work to release that trauma.

—Elly Morrison

Everyday Miracles

The Heavenly Helper

About ten years ago, I woke up one morning feeling extremely nauseated with a terrible headache. Within a few hours, I also experienced double vision. I had a strong intuition that I needed to call an optometrist I knew, who was also a physician. When I called, he got me in for an immediate appointment. He examined my eyes briefly, and said that he could get me in for a CAT scan that same day. I was at the hospital within an hour for the CAT scan and MRI scan.

The brain and spine physician told me I had experienced a spontaneous spinal leak. He said that this phenomenon was extremely rare; only a few people were reported to have experienced it. Despite the rarity of this condition, the doctor said that he knew what to do. He suggested that caffeinated drinks, like coffee and tea, might help me feel better until they could get me into the hospital. He called me the following day to ask if I could wait a couple of days, as he had another serious case happening, and I said okay.

While I waited, I experienced extremely vivid dreams that I still remember to this day. I also experienced waking hallucinations, such as green leafy vines climbing up my bedroom wall. My daughter drove me to the hospital two days later, and stayed

102

with me until they wheeled me into the room where the procedure would be done. The staff assistant helped me lie down on my stomach on a table, and then the nurse attempted to draw blood from my hand to perform a "blood patch," which would patch the leak in my spine.

At the first attempt, the blood wouldn't draw from the vein in my hand. The nurse put the needle in my arm, and the blood still wouldn't flow out. She put the needle in a different place in my arm. The blood didn't flow. I have low blood pressure, and apparently the caffeinated drinks had dehydrated me. I could tell that the nurse was getting worried and frustrated. The only way to seal a spinal leak is to make a blood patch with the patient's own blood, and getting it to flow in sufficient quantities is important, as it assures a more stable patch.

At that point, in my mind's eye, I saw a beautiful angel with wavy brown hair hovering over my back. She conveyed to me that I needed to lower my right arm and dangle it from the edge of the table. So I told the nurse and she agreed. After my arm was dangling, there was a pause when nothing happened, and then my blood started flowing strongly and smoothly, which provided enough blood to seal the leak.

I might add that the hospital staff had forgotten to inform me not to eat anything before the procedure because I would be given I.V. sedation. I did eat beforehand, and so they could not use normal sedation. If I had been unconscious, I would not have been able to tell the nurse how to help get my blood to flow. I am very grateful to the angel, and to the team of doctors and nurses. I was guided and assisted the whole way by spirit.

—*Polly Richter*

Chapter 6

Divine Timing
Signs & Synchronicities

Everyday Miracles

Trust God to Give You a Sign

On October 10, 1979, I lost my brother Jack in a fatal car accident back in my hometown of Waterford, Connecticut. I think it might have been on a Wednesday. I was living in Augusta, Kansas, at the time. That day a mysterious thing happened.

The following weekend, I was supposed to be going to a Beta Sigma Phi Sorority convention. The other members of my sorority indicated that they would be wearing dresses to the convention, so I had bought a new dress for the occasion. One of my sorority sisters came over for a visit and I showed her the beautiful blue dress that I had purchased. As I put the dress back in the closet, the thought went through my head that if I had a funeral to go to, I had a dress to wear. That evening at about 8:00 I received a phone call that my brother Jack had been killed in a car accident. The time of the accident was the exact time that the thought went through my head that I had a dress to wear for a funeral. Instead of going to the convention, I attended my brother's funeral in Connecticut.

About a month after my brother's death, I started having some unusual symptoms, such as nausea and dizziness. I went to see the doctor that had delivered my daughter Andrea. I told him about my symptoms and he basically told me to go home and take some vitamins. I think he believed it was all in my head. Yet I still felt like something was really wrong with me, so I made an appointment with Dr. Varner, an osteopath, and the husband of one of my sorority sisters.

Dr. Varner started out by doing a blood test called an SMA 20. I had a strong feeling that the blood test would not show anything abnormal. I asked him what he was going to do when the blood test came back and didn't reveal anything wrong with me. He promised to do the blood tests free of charge. He then took me to an exam room to check my blood pressure and my heart. Suddenly I felt the need to ask him to check a mole on my back. I had never really looked at my back and I now believe it was Divine Intervention that had caused me to ask about the mole. He found something suspicious and suggested that he would measure it and watch to see if it grew.

I asked him, "Why don't you remove it right now so I don't have to worry about it?" He did as I requested.

Dr. Varner called me on Friday and told me that the blood test didn't show any abnormalities, and wasn't I glad? I think he was trying to humor me, but I said, "I know something is really wrong." He told me to come in at 3:00 that afternoon and he would do the free blood test that he had promised.

When I arrived at his office, he said that he had received the pathology report on the mole from the lab. "What you have is malignant melanoma," he said. The first words out of my mouth were, "Am I going to die?" As I recall, his response was, "I don't think so." I believe he gave me a sedative of some sort to calm me down.

That evening, I drove to a friend's home to tell her that I had just been diagnosed with melanoma. On the way home, I stopped at a stop sign and prayed. I put the situation in God's hands. No matter what happened, I knew that everything would be okay. At the time I had three young daughters, the youngest was only two years old. My children were my greatest concern.

The next morning I woke up with a sense of peace. I felt like a weight had been lifted off my chest. Suddenly the phone rang. I was informed that I had won a drawing at a local store. When I went to pick up what I had won, the prize handed to me was a necklace with a cross on it. I took that as an omen. My other prizes were an ashtray and a bottle of fake champagne.

The following Tuesday I was admitted to the hospital. The surgeon removed a five-centimeter area around the melanoma and took a graft from my leg to fill in the gap. About a month later, I took one of my daughters to see Dr. Varner. While we were in his office, he informed me that my melanoma had been only the thickness of a piece of paper away from being lethal. He also thought that I had ESP and wanted me to get it developed. He told me that if I ever had a premonition about him I was to let him know immediately. My feeling is that it was a miracle that saved my life.

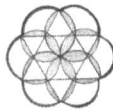

Anyone who is a cancer survivor will be able to relate to the second story I am about to tell. In August of 2007, a month after my daughter left to teach in Malaysia, I was diagnosed with breast cancer. I went through months of chemotherapy, lost all my hair, and had to have weeks of radiation treatment. After all of my treatments were finally done, I was told to have a mammogram screening every six months for several years.

On the way to one of my first appointments after my cancer treatment, I was a little nervous as to what might be found. Driving down the road to my appointment that day, I spotted a rainbow in the distance. I took the rainbow as a sign that everything would be okay—and it was. The mammogram was clear.

Recently, when I went for my annual mammogram, I felt fortunate when it was over that I could just go home again. The following week, however, I received a call to come back in for further testing. Something suspicious was found on the mammogram.

Almost immediately, I said a prayer for a sign that everything was okay. I went out to water the flowers and bushes around the house, and I saw one rainbow after another in the mist of the spray from the garden hose. I knew at that moment that everything was going to be fine.

I also find signs to guide me in my dreams. That night I dreamed that I had cancer in several places in my body. But over the years, I have learned that when I dream something, it means that it will NOT happen. For instance, when I dreamed that my final pregnancy would result in a son (after having three daughters), I knew that I was going to have a fourth daughter.

My appointment for the recheck was at 8:00 the following morning. After the signs I had received as guidance, I almost didn't bother to go in for further testing because I was so sure everything was going to be okay. The radiologist did another mammogram that was more thorough and more painful than the first. I waited for the results right there at the imaging place. Just as I knew it would be, everything was fine, and I was soon on my way home for a great day ahead!

—*Kathy Chasteen*

The Green Card

Four years ago, I was at a party in Blaine, Washington, at a friend's house. It was late and I decided to spend the night instead of driving home after dark. When I awoke in the morning, I noticed that my wallet was missing, which contained my credit cards, drivers license, one hundred dollars in cash—and most important, my "green card." I needed it to cross over the border into Canada where my family lived. I was born and raised in Canada, and my three brothers and sister have always lived there, but I decided to live in the United States.

After many months of searching for my wallet to no avail, I was no longer able to cross the border into Canada to see my family for holidays or other occasions. The cost to apply for another green card and do all the paperwork was exorbitant, so I could not afford to replace it.

As the next four years went by, I became increasingly depressed and worried that if an emergency happened to any of my family members, I would not be able to help them. Then one morning, I received a call from the Blaine Police Department. They asked me to come down to the station. At the time, I couldn't imagine why they would want to see me, and my mind was whirling. It had been four years since I had even visited Blaine.

When I got to the station, I approached the front desk and announced my name and explained that I was asked to come in. The receptionist left the room and quickly returned with a small package for me. I opened the package, and low and behold! There was my wallet still in perfect condition. I anxiously looked inside, assuming all would be gone, only to find that the cash was gone, but my drivers license, credit cards—and most important, my green card—were still there, exactly in the order I had put them inside the wallet four years ago. It was unbelievable … nothing short of a Miracle! Shaking and in shock, I walked back to my car and said a prayer of thanks, with tears in my eyes.

Two months later, in January 2015, I received a call from my brother George's wife informing me that he had just suffered a massive coronary heart attack and couldn't be revived. I was devastated at the news, as I loved my brother very much. We hadn't seen each other for several years—prior to the time my wallet went missing. Sadly, I had been planning to visit him in just two weeks when I got the call.

The service for my brother George was that Friday, so I drove to Vancouver, BC, to the home of George and his family to help his wife Amelia and their son get ready for the service the next day. They told me it was a huge comfort to them to have me there.

The day of the service, the rest of the family arrived; my two remaining brothers, my sister, and many nieces, nephews, and friends—my brother had many.

During this whole ordeal, I was still in a state of shock thinking about that wallet appearing out of nowhere, with the very card I so desperately needed to cross the border into Canada. And it turned up just in the nick of time so I was able to be at my brother's funeral.

Forever grateful and in AWE, I am NOW a TRUE BELIEV-ER IN MIRACLES.

—*Bill Hamar*

Somewhere in Time
A Love Story

Dedicated to Marcia Reimers and Paul Reimers,
without whose friendship my life would be quite different

Spirit knows ... Spirit knows when everything will begin and how it all fits together. The plan for our meeting began many years before Larry and I met. So many details to fit together, one piece here, another piece there. I like to think of it as a whisper that I could almost hear, an idea, a feeling—maybe a whole sentence or a section of a picture. In my late teens, I had a session with a Tarot card reader. I remember quite vividly one piece of information she shared, "Oh my, he really does love you!" She could not tell me who "he" was. It would be many years before I met the man who really does love me.

I will begin the story in 1988. Early in my pregnancy with my second daughter, Natalie, my first husband and I and our toddler Rachel moved to Bellingham from Seattle. We settled down in the Eldridge area. I wanted to meet people and get some exercise, so I found a prenatal class at Bellingham Athletic Club. I discovered another mom in the class that I enjoyed spending time with. Her name was Marcia, and she was a few months ahead of me in her pregnancy. We had fun talking about our pregnancies and other typical mom talk. She brought her daughter Arielle to class with her and I brought Rachel. The girls played together while we stretched and talked. I continued going to the class for a few weeks, but I missed seeing Marcia there. I assumed that she must have had her baby. My experience in class felt different not pairing with Marcia. I found that I was not as motivated to attend, so I began to fill my time with other activities instead. Spirit knows the way and how our lives fit together. It would not be too long before I reconnected with Marcia—at a place that would become my spiritual oasis in Bellingham.

While living in Seattle with my first husband, when Rachel was a toddler, I was introduced to Bellevue Unity Church through my metaphysical study group. As I walked through the doors at Unity, I felt like I had come home from a long trip! When we moved, I was surprised and excited to discover a Unity church in Bellingham. I attended a few Sunday services and a class before my daughter Natalie was born. After a few months went by, I felt an urge to go back to church. I soon became involved in the Youth Education program at Unity, which is where, led by Spirit (and not by coincidence), I found Marcia again. She and her husband Paul and their two girls, Arielle and Shaila, were members at Unity. Our families became close friends. We shared dinners and holidays together, and the girls often entertained us with plays they created. We went on retreats together and helped build each other's houses.

During this time, my love for Spirit and Unity blossomed, and I stepped up to be a Youth Ed Director and then Volunteer Coordinator. My life was full, and fun; I loved being a mom, I

loved my church and friends. However, my marriage was beginning to tailspin. My husband began to stay out until late at night,
and increasingly drank alcohol. When I found out about his affair
with one of his co-workers, I knew that I was worthy of much more
from my husband. I gave him a choice: he could take this opportunity to change and be with me and our two beautiful, sweet
little girls, or leave. He chose to leave.

My Unity family gathered around and supported the girls
and me through the devastating change. I read *The Daily Word*,
practiced affirmations, took classes, and accepted the love of our
church family. I dated a bit, and what I mostly learned from this
experience was that knowing what I don't want in a partner is
equally as powerful as knowing what I do want.

Now that my heart had grown and matured, Spirit knew
the time was right for me to gently get to know a new gentleman.
Someone named Larry Humes, who Paul said might help with
this or that around the church. I could never figure out just who
Larry was even though I knew almost everybody there. That was
part of my job as Volunteer Coordinator.

That Christmas at Unity, I sat in the front row listening to the most beautiful sound of "someone" playing "O Holy
Night" on a French horn (That was Larry). Little did I know that
Larry's attention had been caught by this "cutie" (my nickname)
at church.

That spring, Marcia and Paul had a work party to help them
build an addition on their home. Larry and I were both at the
work party, but we were not on the same crew. We were in such
close proximity! I trust and know that Spirit had more in its plan
than we could anticipate.

Time marched on. The girls were busy with school and sports activities, but we continued to share dinners and celebrate holidays with the Reimer family. We also spent time with family in Seattle. I was struggling to provide for my girls on a meager budget, and I was grateful to their grandparents and my brother for funding sports camps and new school clothes. It was during this time that I realized the best thing I could do for my children was to go back to school to increase my earning potential. So I enrolled in college to get a masters degree in teaching. I decided to focus on schoolwork, self-improvement, and my girls' wellbeing. My priority was to raise healthy, well-educated daughters and provide for their future.

I like to believe that Spirit was ready to change the whisper into a soft-spoken word. I credit my girls with telling me I should get a life and go have some fun, as I had not wanted to date anyone for a few years. I shared my daughters' sage wisdom with Paul and Marcia. Paul (ever the matchmaker) suggested that I meet a guy he knew. I let him know that I was not quite ready for romance in my life. Paul suggested that I just go out to dinner with them and listen to a band playing at the Wild Buffalo. My girls, of course, encouraged me to go. I agreed, with the intention of enjoying a little nightlife.

This part of the story is important. Life had become safe for me, predictable. Life had also become a shade of grey; there was no glow of fire lighting me up inside to help me discover who I was as an educated, athletic, spiritual, adventurous—and single woman.

We three, Paul, Marcia and I, shared a pizza at La Fiamma. Paul introduced me to the guys in the band and I asked them to play "Mustang Sally." I was slightly petrified to be in a nightclub. I certainly didn't want to talk to anybody quite yet. I found a good spot to sit down and listen to the music. My night was made when a cute guy sat on the stool next to me. Maybe this was going to be okay? The band started to play my request, so I had to go out and dance. I believe Spirit took over my mind, and before I knew it, I had asked the cute guy to dance! This was me (with Spirit's support) reminding me that life is fun—Life is a dance!

I like to think of this evening as my "wake-up call." That was the moment when I knew I wanted to meet someone, the right someone. I felt a warm glow, a new sense of worthiness, a desire to understand who I wanted to attract into my life. I made a list of desired qualities, similar interests to share, how this new man may look, and how he could fit into our threesome.

Jump ahead a few months. It is now springtime. The birds are singing, flowers blooming—the season of love! Paul mentions to me again that there is this guy I should meet. I don't say yes, but I don't exactly say no. One Sunday I am uncharacteristically late for church. I see Paul in the front row and slip into a chair behind him. My body instantly has this strange, excited, anxious energy. I realize, without ever having met Larry, that I am sitting next to him. As the service begins, the congregation stands and starts to sing. In my rush to find a seat, I had forgotten to get a hymnal. Larry kindly offers to share his hymnal with me. Spirit smiles.

Larry and I went on our first date a few weeks later. He suggested we go rollerblading at the harbor. It is an exquisite April day. We have fun rollerblading and he asks if I would like to go out on his sailboat. We sail on light wind in Bellingham Bay. Our time together fits like a puzzle, completes a picture that has been forming for sixteen years. I knew when we were quietly enjoying the early spring warmth on the boat that this was good . . . this person felt comfortable, good—even in the quiet, no need to fill space, just be. I knew I could be with this man for the rest of my life.

Larry and I have been together since that first date and will soon celebrate our 15th wedding anniversary.

—*Shari Humes*

The Answer to a Prayer

One Sunday morning, many years ago, when my family and I were living in Brentwood, Tennessee (a suburb of Nashville), we went to the new church that we had joined the previous month. We had been visiting this church for around six months before we became members. On this particular morning, my wife Vicki was teaching her first Bible lesson to a group of women at the church. Just as she started teaching, a woman sitting in the back of the class, who Vicki had never seen there before, started to cry. She thought to herself, "Oh boy, I am in trouble now. I must have said something that upset this lady and they will never let me teach here again. What will I say to John about my mistake?"

Vicki finished teaching the class, and after the other women had left the room, the stranger came up to speak to her.

"You do not know me, but I know you," she said. "Over a year ago, my minister asked me to seek out non-members and invite them to our church. I told him that I was too shy. He then asked if I would pray for someone to come to our church and I said that I would. I live across town about 45 minutes away from here. My job is cleaning offices at night and I clean your husband's office. I have never met your husband, but I see a picture of you and your children on his desk every night. For the past year, I have been getting down on my knees twice a week to pray that you would find my church some day. Today, I visited this church with my sister who goes to your church. When I saw you teaching in this room, I broke out crying to see my prayers being answered. That is the power of prayer. When we ask the universe for anything unselfishly, God always gives it to us."

Joel Goldsmith once said, "You can ask God for anything that is not of this world."

May we never forget to thank God for giving us whatever we ask for that is not of this world. This is the Miracle of the Power of Prayer.

—*John Logan*

Chapter 7

Unexpected Gifts

Everyday Miracles

"Little Things"

The little things are most worthwhile,
A quiet word, a look, a smile,
A lending ear that's glad to share,
Another's thought, another's care.
The little things may seem quite small,
But really mean the most of all.

—Jon Strong

A Gift from Grandma

I never knew my biological father. My parents divorced when I was 9 years old, and after their divorce, I only occasionally saw the man I thought was my father. My parents did the best they knew how when raising us kids, but they probably should never have had children. My sister and I pretty much had to raise ourselves. My father died of alcoholism at the age of 69. At the age of 27, I discovered that he was my sister's biological father but not mine. This came as quite a surprise to me, and I really didn't quite know what to do with this information.

With the encouragement of my husband, I decided I would look for my real father at the age of 36. After weeks of searching, I was told that he had passed away in 1973 from cancer. I was deeply disappointed not to be able to meet him. I knew he had a brother—my true uncle, so I decided I would search for him. My mother was not happy for me to "open this can of worms." She had felt so much guilt about being pregnant with another man's child when she was married to someone else. She didn't want me making inquiries to people in her past. Evidently, I was conceived one weekend at a class reunion. My mother and biological father had gone to the same school and were long-time friends. They were never more than just friends.

My mother had told my biological father that she was pregnant with his child from their one night "reunion," but he didn't believe her. He was married and she was married and my mother didn't feel she could pursue him about being my father any further. Years later he looked my mother up and paid her a visit. He saw a picture of me and knew instantly I was his daughter. My mother told me he had sobbed that day, but whatever he was feeling was never made known. He chose not to make any contact with me. The way my mother put it, "He wouldn't have wanted to upset his family apple cart." The man who helped raise me for nine years knew that I wasn't his real daughter, but accepted me as his own.

I found my biological father's brother (my true uncle) and evidently my father had confided in him that he had conceived a daughter with my mother. When I called my uncle, he and my aunt took me under their wing and invited me to their home to meet three sisters and one brother. That meeting was quite overwhelming. There was no doubt in their minds that I was their true sister. I looked a lot like all of them.

Through the years, my uncle and older sister have spent a lot of time informing me of all the family history and giving me much love and attention. My uncle died in 1994 and I was devastated, as he was like a substitute father. My relationships continue with two of my cousins, my only brother, and my older sister's granddaughter, and I'm especially close with my older sister. All have been blessings in my life. My older sister was raised by our grandmother, my father's mother. She has told me hours of stories about our grandmother. My aunt and uncle were like substitute parents for my sister. She was lucky to have them all in her life.

The first time my older sister visited me at my home, we had some wonderful connecting moments. Above my fireplace mantel is a Jody Bergsma Geese picture, which is the same picture my sister has above her mantel. We both have wooden loons in our homes, as we love watching loons and hearing their sound. We discovered many other things we had in common—grilled cheese on sourdough, walking barefoot on the ocean shore, sending cards to people we love for every occasion, attending open houses on Sundays because we love looking at houses. The list goes on.

Sadly, I never got to meet our grandmother. She died in 1986, the year I started searching for my father. Even though I never met her, I feel deeply connected to her and feel I truly know who she was. I have many pictures of her and endless stories. I fell in love with the woman she was. I aspire to be like her. My father's family has told me that out of all the relatives, I am most like her. I take that as the highest compliment.

My grandmother was born in 1889. Ironically, this was the same year that Unity Church was founded. Since 1980, I have attended Unity Church of Bellingham, where I met my husband (of 35 years) who shares my spiritual beliefs. In her early twenties, my grandmother joined the church and devoutly practiced the Unity teachings. What a progressive woman she was for her day. She raised my father and uncle in Unity. My father was married in the Seattle Unity Church. My grandmother had a special holder for her *Daily Word* and read it each day. My older sister and I were amazed that grandmother and I were both members of Unity. My sister gave me Grandma's holder for my own *Daily Word*. My grandmother's most powerful expression was, "Dear, we must be loving and kind to all people." She was a true example of Unity teaching. I am told that there wasn't a person that didn't love her.

Grandma worked in the millinery department of a major department store. She and my grandfather were lower income people, but grandma knew how to scrimp and save and have enough money to prepare meals for others, help raise three of her grandchildren, make clothes. She even saved money so my sister could learn how to play the piano. She happily did so many things with a positive attitude and a smile on her face, always eager to help a neighbor. She just loved and cared about people. When she worked at the department store, a black woman was pregnant and the workers were invited to a baby shower. That year, my grandmother had gotten my sister a job in the same department store. When my grandmother heard that no one was going to attend this black woman's baby shower, my grandmother took my sister by the hand and said, "Come on honey, we are going to celebrate the birth of a new and perfect child."

My grandmother gave her wedding ring to my older sister when she got married. My sister wore the ring for 40 years and then she gave it to me. I love this ring. The setting has a tiny diamond and a citrine stone etched with a lily. Lilies and lilacs were grandma's favorite flowers. One day I took the ring to be cleaned with some other jewelry. When I got to the jewelry store, the ring was gone. All the other jewelry in my bag was there, but not my grandmother's ring. I was devastated. The bag was not totally zipped closed and the ring must have fallen out.

I searched high and low—in the car, in the grass, in the street. I even went home and searched the house. The ring was nowhere to be found. I was sick to my stomach. I went back to the jewelry store and told them what happened. The owner told me she had an employee who was great at finding things. "She finds everything we lose around here." The employee happened to be in the back room, and she went outside to look for the ring. There in the street she found it, even though I had searched the same area several times. Apparently, a car had run over the ring and it shot out in a different part of the street. The band of the ring was crunched and twisted, but the stone was still in perfect condition and the entire ring was repairable.

At that moment, I understood the importance of my grandmother's influence in my life. The ring is a symbol of my grandmother's strength and love. It was meant for me to always have her spirit with me. I found out later that my grandmother had known that I was another one of her grandchildren. When I look back at my life, I honestly believe that my grandmother has always been watching out for me and protecting me. Sadly, there were several times when I came close to death, but somehow something always saved me. It was my Unity grandmother watching out for me. Whether or not this is true, I choose to believe it.

Recently, I met a woman at the grocery store who noticed my ring and thought it was lovely. When I told her it was my grandmother's wedding ring, she physically jerked back a few times. I thought she was quite odd. The woman told me that she was clairvoyant and that my grandmother was right there with us. She said she could see her, and described exactly what she looked like. She said that my grandmother was very proud of me and hangs out with me a lot. I choose to believe it.

I feel so lucky to have such an honorable blood relative. I feel my grandmother's presence and am so proud to be her granddaughter.

—Kelly Jameson

Listening with Your Heart

A few years back, I was performing the usual evening ritual of walking my dog around the block. Always the busy lady, I was rushing through the walk and ready to go home. As I passed by the front yard of an elderly neighbor, Rose, I stopped to look at her house and knew in that moment I needed to visit with her. Rose answered the door and cordially invited both me and my dog inside. She offered me something to drink and smiled warmly as she asked me to sit on her sofa. We chatted about everyday things for a few minutes and then she brought up the subject that had been on my mind for several days – her open-heart surgery.

Rose had mentioned to me a couple of weeks earlier that her heart problems were increasing and that she had been scheduled for surgery in Seattle in the near future. And now I learned that tomorrow was the day. I looked closely at Rose and noticed that she had lost weight, there were dark circles under her eyes and she seemed very agitated. I know that spirit was guiding me when I asked her to tell me more about her past and her family. She brightened immediately and excused herself from the room for a few minutes. On her return, Rose had an armful of books and magazines, which she placed on the coffee table as she sat next to me.

The next two hours with Rose were a mixture of deep conversation, laughter, stories, tears, and talk of her family and their history in Whatcom County. I can say that the time flew by and I was surprised to see that it was now after 10:00. Since I knew Rose needed her rest for her journey and surgery the next day, I offered to help straighten up the room and put things away. As we finished, Rose walked to the china cabinet in the dining room and brought out a small figurine. As we walked to the door, she told me the history of this heirloom piece and then placed it in my hand. She told me that my visit with her was such comfort and delight that she felt the need to reciprocate and share something valuable with me. I was deeply touched and remember telling her that everything would be fine with the surgery and to please call me as soon as she returned home from the hospital.

Rose never returned to her sweet little home in our neighborhood. She passed away during the surgery. Her house was eventually sold and there have been three families in and out of it since she left. What I take away from that final evening we shared is that the most important listening comes through an open heart, not with our ears. I thank spirit for telling me to slow down that evening and reach out to Rose. And I am so grateful that I listened.

—Erin O'Reilly

A Final Gift of Words

My mom died on January 29, 2016. Her name was Ann, and she had gone into a different world long before her body left, too. Her decline into dementia started with a cerebral vascular incident —a blood clot that shut off supply to part of her brain. It probably did not last more than two minutes, but it was long enough to do damage. That part of the brain tissue died and the rest slowly followed over the next four years.

I was born when mom was 19; my brother, when she was 20; and my sister on her 21st birthday. Three more siblings followed over the next sixteen years. She was a stay-at-home mom with her hands very full taking care of her children. In my sophomore year of college, she decided to get a nursing degree, and after graduating with honors, mom had a long successful career as a registered nurse. After her retirement, she continued to tutor nursing students for several more years. She was always learning and exploring things, and encouraged her children to do the same. She told us we could be and do anything we wanted in life.

Ann was a caretaker—of her children and grandchildren, of her mother who died of cancer, of a spouse who also died of cancer, of her patients and neighbors—and even when she moved into the care center, she looked after others.

Mom always had the right words to say. When I think of her, I often think of her words of wisdom, and not just the usual "momisms" (e.g. "If you can't say anything nice, don't say anything at all" or "You will thank me for this someday"). I started playing scrabble with Mom at a very young age and delighted in learning new words—she let me play with an open dictionary by my side. Mom read to us kids most nights at bedtime when we were young. Our home was filled with books, and we all had library cards before we started grade school. Mom and I had the same taste in authors and stories, and we spent hours discussing books over the years. She introduced me to Steinbeck when I was 8 (still one of my favorite authors). Later in life, our discussions included spiritual beliefs, as I had become interested in energy work, Reiki specifically, and was seeing some wonderful healing results, both personally and with clients. Mom was Catholic to the end, yet she believed in a bigger view and a loving god.

When my mom's dementia started to present in more major ways, her biggest frustration was not being able to find her words. She would trail off a sentence and just stare into space, frustrated. It made her angry. She could no longer share her opinions, or visit with a grandchild, or even follow a discussion, let alone lead one. As the disease progressed, she quit reading, one of the biggest losses of all.

She required care beyond what we could give her on our own, and so we found a place for her in a dementia care facility with wonderful, gentle staff. I made the eight-hour trip to see her every 6 to 8 weeks over the next two years. During my visits, I would talk to her normally, updating her on my life or the latest book I was reading, just like we used to talk together. She would look at me and smile, maybe nod now and then.

The day came when she could not recognize me, or any of her children, and she no longer verbalized anything more than a grunt. She spent her days in her own world, somewhere unreachable by any of us. I still visited her all the same, because I knew who SHE was. And I still talked to her as I once did, but now she would look around the room or nod off to sleep. Our visits became just sitting together holding hands.

My last trip to visit Mom was at Thanksgiving, two months before her death. I arrived a little before lunchtime, and sat down beside her at the dining room table to help her eat her lunch. It was her habit to take a nap after lunch, so we went to her room. I tucked her into bed and lay down with her, cuddling and holding her, talking gently until she fell asleep. I got up quietly without disturbing her. I kissed her forehead, and told her I missed her so much, and that I loved her. I got my coat and purse, and just as I put my hand on the door knob, I heard her say, "I love you too, honey." She was sitting up in bed, smiling at me. I went back, knelt down and hugged her, and then she was gone, once again, into her own world.

As I sat in my car crying, I knew my mom had given me one last gift—her gentle words. Her final goodbye.

—*Sally Ledgerwood*

Brotherly Love

In 2009 my youngest brother Greg left his body here on Earth when he was 50 years young. He was loved by almost all who had the opportunity to interact with him. I am certain that smiles still break forth and joyful tears flow down the cheeks of many when thoughts of him come to mind. Truly gregarious, he was so aptly named. He sizzled with zeal each and every day, finding joy in taking time to savor all of his experiences. So many of our family stories illustrated his exuberant perspective—the way Greg appreciated the fullness of life's offerings.

One day many years ago, while still in his late teens, Greg was bustling out the front door of our family home. He found me, his oldest sister, sitting alone in contemplation on our front porch step feeling despondent. I had to return home, once again, because I was dealing with yet another round of serious debilitating illness. Suspending his own plans, Greg stopped and sat down with me. I will never forget how he reached me then and there. He bettered my remaining years with this sweet, soft offering of practical advice that helped me navigate the seas of my chaotic family life.

"Leslie," he said, "when the waves of life become dark or choppy, take care of you. First."

Yes, I had heard that encouragement many times, from many wise and loving sources. But I truly only received this wisdom for the first time from my brother, because of how he said it to me. As he spoke the words, he put his hand over his heart and then embraced his whole body to indicate the importance of caring for my entire being. This visual was just what I needed—it may seem like such a small thing to do, but it changed my life. I will always be grateful for his lovely, gentle, life-giving gifts to me:

The gift of Time

The gift of Grace

The gift of Presence

By being there for me so perfectly and completely, and speaking those clarion heartfelt words of truth, my brother Greg empowered me in a way I will never forget. I will always cherish that moment. I miss him. And yet his gracious gifts flow eternally.

—*Bell Spence*

Chapter 8

Blessings at Heaven's Door

Everyday Miracles

A Song for Mom

When I was a child, my mother nurtured my God-given talents in music and the fine arts with lessons and opportunities. Like most children, I hated practicing, but I loved music and would sit at the piano and pick my favorite songs from the hymnbook or any other songbook and sing and play for hours. Looking back, I am sure my mother must have been smiling and dreaming her dreams for me even then.

As a teen, however, my musical tastes and other interests began to change. The hopes and dreams my mother had for me were not the same ones I was choosing for myself. At the age of 18, I left my parents' home in California and moved to Washington State to assert my own influence over my life.

Along with the move, I left behind my religious upbringing, and for the most part, my musical talent lay dormant while I explored the places and people in my new life. Although I spoke with my parents regularly, I felt my mother's disappointment, and we never seemed to develop that bond that some adult children are able to find with their parents.

However, God did have a plan for my life, and by late 1987 I was married, with a beautiful 4-year-old daughter and a second on her way. My husband and I had found our way back to church, and I was even singing in a small choir. It also became evident that year that something was not right with Mom. Physically, she seemed healthy enough, but her speech pattern was slower, and she had a tendency to repeat what had just been said.

Trips to the doctor resulted only in frustration for her family. "She's fine...quite healthy," said one doctor after another. Finally, however, in late 1988, the doctors could no longer say they detected nothing amiss, and began more in-depth testing. By this time, her speech consisted of short sentences and single syllables. The doctors began to talk about the possibility of ALS – Lou Gehrig's disease.

For months I had been calling at least once a week just to keep in touch, but by early 1989, the phone conversations with Mom were becoming pretty one-sided, and her tears of frustration over not being able to communicate tore at my heart. The 1200 miles that separated us might as well have been 12,000.

I flew to Los Angeles for a long weekend visit in February of that year, taking along my 8-month-old daughter. By coincidence, while I was there, the doctors finally gave her a diagnosis: Progressive Pseudo Bulbar Palsy (a neuromuscular disease with symptoms and patterns similar to ALS). There were no treatments, no cures. Life expectancy averaged 2-4 years from the onset of symptoms.

Mom was in a downhill slide now with nothing to stop it. As the disease ran its course, she was no longer able to chew or to swallow. By early July, it was apparent she had just a few months left. My heart ached to be with her and Dad. After all these years, all I wanted was to let her feel the love that had lay in my heart unspoken.

One evening, feeling overwhelmed by it all as I drove to town, it all began to come out. I pulled off the road and the words and music that had been dormant inside me for so long poured onto a sheet of scrap paper. Later, at home, I sat at the piano and added accompanying chords to the lyrics and melody playing over and over in my head and heart.

So there it was in written form, saying everything I wanted her to know. But would she like it or was it too close to what she was experiencing? Maybe I was being too bold by acknowledging this Truth that seemed to come through me without provocation or forethought. It felt SO right to me ... a message from God ... but could she hear it and feel that same Truth?

Then it was time to risk it all. I wrote her a letter and included the words to my song. Dad called the day they got the letter. Mom loved it and wanted to hear the music. Could I make a tape and send it to her?

I decided to make a video, including footage of my children, and put the song on at the end. Dad called again after they received it. She loved it, and was playing it for everyone who came to visit.

On August 8th, Mom turned 63, and went into a Hospice facility. She wanted no life sustaining interference, only to be comfortable. Hospice could only keep her for a week, then sent her home with a prognosis of 2-4 weeks.

I decided it was time to go there. I made arrangements to fly south, this time taking both daughters with me. Mom now needed round the clock care and Dad needed someone to be there to help.

We flew from Seattle to Los Angeles on August 17th. It was a long day. Our late afternoon flight was delayed two hours. When we finally arrived at LAX, my brother, who was scheduled to pick me up, had been delayed. He showed up just at the same time the baggage came through. Then, heading back from the airport, across the expanse of this huge city, we missed a freeway change and found ourselves lost, spending another 10-15 minutes finding our way to the right onramp.

We finally arrived at Mom and Dad's around midnight. My daughters were sound asleep. We plunked them into already-prepared beds. My brother said goodnight to Mom, told her he loved her, then left to find his way to his own home.

Now, at last, it was my turn to be with Mom. Her face was sunken and gray. I stroked her hair and told her I loved her. I held her hand as Dad filled me in on the past few hours. Then, he asked me to sing her the song I had written for her. The rest of the world disappeared as I softly sang:

> *I see, I hear, I feel you dying*
> *And part of me is dying with you.*
> *I see, I hear, I feel you crying*
> *And part of me is crying with you.*
> *Our lives grow in a circle,*
> *On and on it goes.*
> *Winter turns to springtime,*
> *New seasons still unfold.*
> *I see, I hear, I feel you living,*
> *And part of you will always live in me.*
> *I see, I hear, I feel your loving,*
> *And always I'll be loving you.*

As I finished, Mom's breathing softened and she passed gently from this life into God's hands. Whenever I remember that night, I thank God for showing me the way home, and I thank Mom for waiting for me to get there.

—*Marcia Reimers*

There Are Many Mansions

I became very close to my mother after my father had died when I was 22. I wanted to help her financially, because my father had not wanted my mother to work outside the home. Back in those days the husband needed to be the "good provider." So my brother bought our family's summer cabin on the lake with enough cash that she could buy a condo and live on just her social security without paying rent or a mortgage. She bought a condo in Bellevue, about a mile and a half away from my home in Redmond, Washington.

Mom was a welcome companion on many of my adventures with friends during the years after my father's passing. She and I went on some trips together, and she came along to the ski resort where I taught and spent weekends. Her good humor and easygoing personality fit in with most of my activities. When I spent time on my own, I felt guilty leaving her alone, even though she had her church friends to keep her company.

By the time I was 39 or 40, my mother was being treated for skin cancer and it had begun to spread inward. I drove her to Virginia Mason Hospital in Seattle for treatments on Fridays, and arranged for "Van Go" (a local shuttle service for the disabled and seniors) to take her from Bellevue to Seattle and back on the other days. After two years of various treatments, the cancer had spread to her lungs. She was very thin, and the doctors said she would not be able to have surgery at her age, 82. I was in shock and denial.

An end-of-life hospice team came to her condo for visits. The hospice nurse told me that mother would go unconscious soon, and said I could give her little morphine pills under her tongue to ease the pain. I called my brother and his wife, who was in medical school, and asked them to come because I knew they would want to be with her, and also I needed their help. I cried most of the days while I stayed with her, and slept on the couch so I could be nearby.

Before she went unconscious, mother told us she wanted us to have a wake. We agreed to do that for her. I asked her to let me know that she was "okay" after she passed. I had gotten the idea to do that from Terry Cole Whittaker, a Church of Religious Science minister I had heard speak at the Seattle Unity Church. Terry shared with us that she had asked her loving aunt to give her a sign before she passed away, and said that she later received a "message" in the form of an emotion and great energy that made her feel like she wanted to do cart wheels.

Friends at Unity of Bellevue helped me to plan the wake for my mother at my new home in Redmond. The morning of the wake, I was cleaning the house and puttering around in silence getting ready for the memorial, which was to be at 2:00 that afternoon. I was lost in thought, just finishing the cleaning. In my living room, there was a bay window with an uncovered cushion on the seat. The fabric I had picked out to cover the cushion rested on the seat, as I had not yet taken it to the seamstress. So I got down on my knees in front of the window and started wrapping the fabric around the cushion, when all of a sudden, the window turned into a different window. I had a vision of a very large window with gold velvet drapes. I can hardly describe the feeling that came over me. It was an incredible feeling of Love and well-being.

The vision lasted for only seconds. I wanted it to last longer, but when I tried to make it last, it ended. Then I remembered how my mother had loved and often shared with me the passage, "In my father's house there are many mansions." I knew that this beautiful gold window was her way of letting me know she was okay.

I felt peaceful and calm. The rest of the day I was not sad, and the wake with our family and friends was wonderful. A piano player brought his keyboard. Many shared kind words about my mother. We made a big circle and sang Alleluia to *Pachelbel's Canon*.

I still miss my mother, and I still talk to her—28 years after her passing. My mother used to say that there is just a veil between us and our deceased loved ones. I know that scientists are now thinking there may be parallel universes. I do think and hope I will see her or feel her presence again. I like to think of her as one of my guardian angels.

—*Beatrice C. Raymond (Gibbs)*

First a "Good-bye," Then a "Hello!"

A Remembrance to My Beloved Shih Tzu

Rusty was my constant companion for 15 years. I knew he was aging, but I chose to be in denial most of the time. At the end of his life, his health problems were related to his treatment for an acute allergic reaction. I rationalized it by thinking that we'd weather the storm and everything would be back to normal.

During a mid-morning trip doing errands, I was driving down the street behind a supermarket. There were no other cars ahead of me, but a seagull stood right in the middle of the street in front of my car and refused to move. I would inch the car forward, but he kept repositioning himself into the middle of the street. Suddenly, he flew up toward my windshield, along with two other seagulls. They were flapping their wings in perfect synchronization. I was so stunned that I stopped the car. Immediately, a huge booming voice came from the back of the car saying, "We will be accompanying Rusty to the afterlife!" I was temporarily immobilized, and then the gulls flew away. Oddly enough, no one was on the street behind me. It was as if time had stopped. I became numb, but I went ahead and finished my errands.

When I arrived home, I saw that Rusty was getting worse. I called my daughter and we took him to the emergency animal hospital together. He needed hydration, but with his heart murmur, that presented a challenge. He would need special care at the hospital. The veterinarians called periodically to give me updates on Rusty. Suddenly, I had a vision of his Core Star rising. It was so bright it blinded me. I then heard him say, "I had to go Mom. I just hurt too much. I love you." The animal hospital called me right at that moment, and said that he had passed. Several days later Rusty came to me in a dream. He said, "Remember Mom, I'm just in the room next door."

It has been said that your pet will choose his successor before crossing over. Five months later, I was online aimlessly looking for another Shih Tzu. I decided it had to be the total opposite of Rusty—a white female. I found myself scrolling on e-Bay through a long list of Shih Tzu's. Then, suddenly, a white female came onto the screen. I casually looked her over and immediately dismissed her with an, "I'm not ready yet." I tried to continue scrolling, but the screen froze!! I looked at her and she stared back at me, as if to say, «Here I am!" The screen remained frozen. I wrote down her information and the phone number. That released the screen, so I could continue scrolling. But I didn't look at many more dogs. Suffice it to say that I've had Clair for 13 months now. Another example of Divine Cosmic Intervention.

—*Judy Milton*

'Til Death Do Us Part

For Karen

"Three down . . . seven letters. This one begins with a p," my father says, looking up from the page into my mother's eyes. His voice is warm and encouraging as he reads the clue: "Name of flower." My mother furrows her brow in concentration for a moment, then opens her eyes wide and looks at him. To my surprise she nails it: "Petunia," she says, in her weak but determined voice. My father gives his crossword prodigy a little kiss and puts away the book as the staff nurse rolls a monitoring cart into the room.

"Morning," she says cheerily. The nurse maneuvers the cart along the bed railing, careful not to jostle her delicate patient, and wraps my mother's arm in the cuff. My father watches intently, as if witnessing this ritual for the first time. He is eager to hear the latest reading. He nods approvingly. The medication is working.

So far we have succeeded in getting "Saint Madge" through the day without much pain. My mother was sainted for her grace under fire by my brother-in-law long before these dark night trials. Today is one of her "good days." She is alert yet relaxed; her gray eyes are steady, not restless and searching as they often are when she slips into the void. I had applied her favorite lipstick that morning and brushed her glossy white hair. For a moment, it seems as if Rose Magdalyn (her given name) might suddenly step out of her wheelchair and walk again perfectly, without paralysis. We all prayed for such a miracle.

The woman asleep in the bed next to my mother's had been admitted to the nursing home the previous week. Her son now enters the room quietly and nods hello as he slides a chair to his mother's bedside. "It's a miracle she's still here," he says, tearing up with emotion. "Thank God she survived!" He goes on to explain the surgical procedure that had saved his mother's life. My father and I smile at him sympathetically and exchange knowing looks. After endless suffering and hellish ups and downs, my mother's escape from death now seemed anything but miraculous. There was a time when my father—Tag, as my mother and their friends called him (a nickname he preferred to Merlin), would have eagerly shared his own miracle story.

It happened in March of 1999. My parents were retired and living their dream in a golf community in Florida. One morning, my dad finished watering the lawn and was just about to leave for the golf course when something called him back into the house. He was surprised to find their pet finch out of its cage and flitting about the room. Then he saw Madge lying on the floor, still breathing, but unconscious.

"Imagine if I hadn't gone back in!" he would say, and go on to describe the harrowing events that followed: 911, the ambulance ride, and the awful news that my mother had suffered a brain aneurysm. The surgeon gave my father twenty minutes to make the agonizing decision whether to helicopter his wife to Jacksonville

Hospital for emergency surgery or let her die. Desperate not to lose her, he consented to the operation. There was hope, based on what the doctor had said, that she would be able to enjoy a pleasant, if more limited, life.

The doctor's prognosis after performing the surgery was far from hopeful. My mother was left in a comatose state on life support in the critical care unit, completely paralyzed on the left side. Once she regained consciousness, she would be able to recognize us and communicate, but she would never regain use of her limbs. She might live another year, maybe two.

In the weeks that followed her "brain event," my mother slowly found her way back to us. My father became her constant companion, her mooring in the fog, as she flickered in and out of consciousness. My sister Karen, who lived in Jacksonville, was essentially on call 24/7. I flew down from Indiana University during the spring break. Not a day passed without family and friends coming to visit my mother. She was blessed to have so many who loved her and prayed for her recovery. Gradually, she regained the ability to speak and swallow food and was transferred to a care facility where she would start her new life.

One year later, it seemed possible to believe that Mom would defy the odds and return to us whole. But sadly, the aneurysm had caused irreversible damage. Though lucid for extended periods, she often slipped into a world much like the past, where she led a full and busy life—or ventured into stranger realms. My dad, of course, wanted none of this! At such times he would do his best to reel her back to the here and now. Though distressed about her crippled body, stiffly wrapped in splints, my mother bore her suffering with dignity. She believed that she would recover from this "terrible disease," as she called it, never grasping the truth of her condition. My father always encouraged her in this belief.

It was a blessing that my mom was able to escape reality, though this freedom came at the expense of her personality. She was not "all there." To some people, even her closest friends, my mother had essentially died. But to our family, she was still very much in this world. We embraced her as she was. The aneurysm may have blunted her critical faculties, but the softening of her edges enabled my mother to receive love and support in a way she never had. She was a self-reliant woman who had served others graciously, so often putting the needs of others ahead of her own.

Sad as it was, the change in my mother gave my parents a second chance at love. Madge became the center of Tag's universe. She even trumped golf! He doted on her like an infatuated lover, and she responded to his affection by living far longer than we imagined possible. My mom had sacrificed much to make my dad a success. Now their roles had reversed. My dad stepped into his caretaker role with enthusiasm, proudly wheeling Madge down the hall in the parade of wheelchairs. Friendly and outgoing by nature, he was popular at "the home." He was always ready with a joke for the staff. But he kept a close watch on things, and if he saw any sign of negligence, my father made it known.

Seven years passed. After fighting for every new day of life for Madge, Tag could no longer fulfill his duty. One night when climbing into bed, he struck his head and blacked out. The next morning he phoned my sister. Alarmed by the sound of his voice, she called 9-11. He had suffered a stroke. Now our dad would begin his own slow journey to recover from a brain injury. He had lost the ability to walk, or speak, or eat—as if to bear my mother's cross for her. My dad was admitted to a rehabilitation center to begin therapy, but after weeks of treatment he showed little improvement and was soon to realize his worst nightmare. He was admitted as a resident at the nursing home. And so began my parents' courtship in wheelchairs.

The staff supported this romance by wheeling Tag down the corridor, mornings and afternoons, to visit Madge. My sister Karen worked the system to free up space for our parents to become roommates. That's how I found them when I next visited. My father was sitting in his wheelchair alongside my mother's bed, gently holding her "good hand." At this point, my parents' caretaker/patient roles had essentially reversed. Now, my mother, attentive to her deaf and mute partner's helpless condition, rallied all her strength to interpret the words my father struggled to communicate. She became his voice and ears.

Despite their limitations, my parents found great comfort in one another. They shared a deep bond from having lived together "for better or for worse" all the way to the golden years. No doubt the trial of their lives was the loss of my brother, at age 41, to a brain tumor. It was my mother who kept vigil at his bedside in the final weeks. Now after a bittersweet chapter of life at the nursing home, my father's loving partner relapsed with a bout of pneumonia and began slipping out to sea.

Once again, my dad was faced with a decision about life support for my mom. Years earlier, she had relapsed into a critical state and was ambulanced to the hospital. The doctor advised my father to prepare for the end. He refused to believe it possible that it was "her time," but consented to let her go. The doctor greeted our family outside my mother's room at the hospital. She explained to us that she would go speak with my mother before we said our final goodbyes. There was nothing more they could do for her. We were shocked by my mom's response: "What makes you such an expert?" Only my dad seemed to understand why she would choose to live. And so the tubes went back in ...

Now, five years later, the situation was different. Tag could no longer take care of Madge. He was ready for her to leave the world of suffering. So when asked about life-sustaining measures, he shook his head, no, and consented to the final step—hospice. Our dear mother was transferred to a peaceful sanctuary where she was lovingly cared for by a team of angels.

On the day my mother was wheeled out the door of the nursing home, my father became a "difficult patient." He howled like a wild animal trapped in a cage. We appealed to the director to admit him to hospice so he could spend my mom's final days with her. By that point, he had developed a host of diseases. But according to the doctors, he did not qualify as a terminal case. He was expected to live a year or more. Miraculously, within a matter of days, he succeeded in finding a way to make himself a hospice candidate. His vital organs were shutting down.

For a married couple to be admitted to hospice and share a room was unprecedented at the center. The staff quickly assembled a bed for my father and placed it beside my mother's. The nurse kindly positioned my parents to face one another and feel each other's presence. Sedated with morphine, they would never again experience pain.

On Monday night, April 4th at 10:45pm (one day after his admission) my father breathed his final breath and preceded his beloved wife of 63 years into the afterlife. The following morning my sister went to visit our mother, who lingered on. Ever humorous, Karen said to her, "Hurry up Mom, Dad is waiting for you!" Utterly exhausted, my sister drove home and soon fell asleep. At 2:15pm the phone rang. It was a hospice nurse. Fifteen hours after my father departed, my mother joined him in heaven.

Our parents' passing together was a blessing to my family, and a beautiful testament to the power of my parents' love. I have since heard many similar stories about life partners who leave the world within hours or days of their beloved.

—Kendra Langeteig

Chapter 9

Between Heaven and Earth
Life Beyond the Veil

Everyday Miracles

The Day I Went to Heaven

On October 16, 1976, I had gone home for lunch and was on my way back to work at a Ford dealership in Bellingham, Washington. When I got to Slater Road and I-5, I had to wait to cross the I-5 northbound lanes to get to the southbound lanes (at that time, there were no freeway overpasses). It was a Canadian holiday so traffic was heavy.

My Pinto hatchback was a stick shift and it didn't move as quickly as an automatic. Just as I started driving across the first northbound lane, a speeding car came over a small hill from I-5 and broadsided me from the second lane. The driver was going 65 mph (the speed limit was 55 mph). I wasn't wearing a seatbelt at the time because they weren't mandatory back then, so the impact of the collision threw me over to the passenger seat and back to the driver's seat. The steel bar that went over the roof of the Pinto and came down on each side saved my life; also, if I had worn a seatbelt, it would have resulted in more serious injuries or death.

My car was pushed 200 feet down the freeway from the impact of the collision before it came to a stop. I do not remember feeling the impact or seeing anything except sudden darkness, and then I was whirling around and around and went up into a tunnel. Once inside the tunnel, I was still and the tunnel was whirling around me. It was then that I saw a beautiful gold light and many figures waiting and welcoming me. As I moved closer and closer to them, there was such a beautiful feeling of peace and acceptance, and I wanted so badly to be there with them.

The figures were dressed, some in white robes, and some looked like they had on slacks and shirts, but all were white and elusive. There was a special feeling of closeness and spiritual knowing between myself and the angelic figures. There were no words spoken, but I felt we were communicating from soul to soul. No words were needed, as we were like one universal being. I felt like everything and everybody I had ever loved was there greeting me.

Just as I thought that I was there with them, I found myself being pulled backwards down that tunnel I had gone up in. The tunnel was spinning around me and I was still; then I was spinning and the tunnel was still. As I looked up, the beautiful light was getting farther and farther away, and I felt a sense of disappointment at being pulled away from it.

All of a sudden, I was looking down at myself in the car. Two guys in a blue pickup were running toward my car and I saw a State Patrol car drive up. The officer got out of his car and went over to check my pulse; I was breathing, but totally unconscious. There was no pain or emotion about anything that was going on, just the sense of watching and knowing who was there. (The State Patrolman was a guy I had gone to high school with.)

I heard the siren from the ambulance racing toward the scene, and then I watched the paramedics carefully lifting me out of the car, sliding me onto the stretcher, and putting me in the ambulance. I heard them calling St. Joseph Hospital ER and talking to the doctor on staff. I do not remember anything more until a week later, when I heard my family doctor say, "Get her out of here!" I heard the defibrillator being used on the patient in the bed next to me, because their heart had stopped.

The next day, the State Patrolman stopped by the hospital to check to make sure I was okay and had regained consciousness. He was surprised when I told him that I remembered how he had arrived at the scene of the accident and checked my pulse. And then the two guys in the blue pickup truck came by to see me and they were shocked that I recognized them.

The following day, the ambulance driver and paramedics stopped by, and when I told them that I had watched them the whole time, they said there was no way I could have remembered them, because I was unconscious. But sure enough, I did.

I was diagnosed with three broken ribs and a concussion, which was a miracle in itself. It was amazing that I even survived, because the speeding car had hit me right on the driver's door. I was in some pain with the broken ribs, but after a couple of weeks, I was able to return to work. I was 39 years old when this accident happened. Thirty years have passed since that day, and I will never forget the beauty, peace, and tranquility of what I saw and felt and how that vision has changed my life spiritually.

—*Zella Chapman*

The Keeper of the Scrolls

Since childhood I have been going out of body with my Guides, and after a near death experience in the Clearwater River in Idaho at the age of 14, I can occasionally go out of my body at will. I have visited a cave of pink crystals several times, returning just to appreciate its beauty. When I was young, my guides often took me to another place of music, crystals, and abstract forms somewhere out in the universe, where the abstract forms took on the movement of the music, as if they were one. It was so beautiful and the sound was a heavenly symphony led by sounds of flutes. Sometimes I would dance on the crystals until I felt like I was one with the movement and sound. It made my heart rejoice. In this place I knew that this music bridged the gap between the physical and the divine. One time the Angels came and danced with me there. I know that this is the place where great composers come to get their music so the world can hear it, too.

Those experiences were child's play compared to another place I have visited many times. This place feels like it is way out in space, in another galaxy. I travel there very quickly, racing beyond hundreds of stars that look like they're leaving a trail as I pass by them. I can see a planet ahead of me, and before I know it, I am flying straight up in the air, maybe a mile, until I come to a large cave. I can't be sure of the surroundings because all I am able to see in detail is the rocks and plant-life around the opening of the cave and the upper part of the cliff. The opening in earth distance appears to be about a block wide and 15 to 20 feet high. The cave appears dark from outside, but I find that I can see clearly when I step inside, where I am met by the guide, who wears a long silvery blue robe. He always seems to know why I have come to see him, even when I myself don't know why I have come. He is my teacher and I love him. I call him the Keeper of the Scrolls. There are hundreds, maybe thousands of scrolls in this place.

The first time I visited this place, the Keeper showed me that the oldest scrolls were on the far left and the latest ones were on the far right. Somehow they are also arranged by topic. He told me that I was welcome to read them. I replied that I would have to live forever to read them all. I could see clearly enough to know they are written in some strange form of hieroglyphics and not in any earthly form of written communication. I also realized that he does not talk with his mouth but uses his thoughts to communicate with me, and somehow I always know what he is thinking. This was not a new process to me, as I had experienced this with my guides; it's a form of communicating through knowingness in the heart, instead of a hearing with the ears.

After the welcoming and the tour, on that first visit, he took me to the far left of the cave and said, "Let us begin at the beginning." He taught that in the beginning nothing existed anywhere. Although there was nothing, there was potential everywhere waiting to be thought, a huge Cosmic Pool of Love that did not know itself until out of that potential came the first spark of awareness—

"I AM." That awareness began to play with the potential until it became the Creative Force most earthlings call GOD. It created galaxies, universes, solar systems with suns and planets; nature, including earth, water, plants, animals, and everything needed for life. Then God, the Creator, extended himself and created humankind. Therefore, since humans were created in God's image, we are one with God and can also play with the potential forces to create whatever we choose.

That day was the first time I realized that we create with our thoughts whether they are love based or fear based. That is what we do, regardless of whether we know it or not. Humans underestimate the power of their mind. I learned that Mental Creation begins with imagination, and then with interest and emotional attachments our thoughts become physical creations, or manifestations. Our actions and reactions have an influence on the process. This is true whether our creative emotions are loving or fearful. If we don't like our creations, we can always choose again, but that is difficult if we don't know we are the one creating our life.

On another visit to the Keeper of the Scrolls, I wanted to know how I could be sure of spiritual Truths. I was very young when my guides began to reassure me that my mother's beliefs of hell, fire, and damnation were not God's Truth, but it was unclear how to know what God's Truth was. The Keeper said the Scrolls teach that every person that walked the earth during any time period has the Truth within their soul or higher self because we are all one with God. We also were given free will, and most who currently walk this earth are believers in fear and separation. Another issue he shared is that the earth is not only a place of free will, but it also allows for souls of different levels of growth to interact and influence each other. To know Truth on Earth, one must have a passionate desire, an attitude of seeking Truth.

Another lesson from the scrolls is that in many places in the universe, the inhabitants are of the same frequency, level of growth, and shared purpose. They are likely to have the same outlook on life and are much more aware of their oneness with each other than we are here on earth. Here on earth our free will allows humans to have different beliefs and experiences that often create conflict. This led to Adam's and Eve's "Knowledge of Good and Evil," as told in the Old Testament of the Bible. This resulted in separation and fear as well as freedom and choice. To know Truth on Earth, one must have a passionate desire, an attitude of seeking, and be flexible enough to lay aside any false beliefs that block our knowingness. I learned that no matter what life brings, all experiences have lessons and are opportunities for growth. The possibilities are limitless, so I have learned to ask myself what a certain experience is trying to teach me.

What I learned from the scrolls that day reminded me of the use of the term "acquired conditioning" in the Taoist I Ch'ing translated by Thomas Cleary. Acquired conditioning includes many unconscious beliefs and programming we have picked up from our families, friends, schools, churches, and life in general. It explains how we can have false beliefs that block the experience and development of most humans. This conditioning creates fear, guilt, shame, and separation from our true self. Forgive yourself. Let go of limiting beliefs. Make an effort to see things differently with an expression of LOVE in your mind, heart, and soul. Knowing spiritual Truth has been a strong desire for me. I ask Spirit for help and guidance and continue to seek Love, Wisdom, Peace and Truth and believe that you will find it.

Another basic concept in the scrolls is that it speaks of the Higher Mind and the fragmented or dissociated mind instead of the mind and the ego. In Truth, they are one. But the scrolls say that if they were not dissociated, life on earth would appear to us as a game, because we would always see the whole picture. It teaches that the fragmentation occurred so that the Higher Mind could learn from observing physical experience, and the fragmented mind could react to experience and intuitions. The total Mind is Love. Listen to the intuitions from your Higher Mind, and be flexible enough to lay aside any false beliefs that may block your Knowingness.

–Emma Jones

Sailing with an Angel

In 2010 my sister Lois Joy finally succumbed to a serious infection and passed away in the hospital. By her side was her husband Ralph who, in his early eighties, always attended to her every need. A few months later, the family had a celebration for her life and spread her ashes in the waters of Puget Sound, where she had lived the last 30 years of her life.

A year later, Ralph decided that it was time to leave the house he and my sister had built together when they settled in Kingston, Washington. He planned to move into a trailer at his son Scott's home in Sequim near Seattle. It was a very practical decision, but one that I am sure took an emotional toll on him. His family in the area organized the move. I came over from Bainbridge Island to help with the move as well, and with all of us working together, we soon had Ralph settled into his cozy trailer.

During my trip home to Alkai beach from Sequim that evening, I had the strangest encounter on the ferry that connects Bainbridge Island with Seattle. It was a blustery evening aboard the ferry. I love riding the ferry and enjoy having the wind in my face on the open deck. As I was walking around the upper deck of the ferry, I noticed, out of the corner of my left eye, a figure moving toward me. When I was in officer candidate school in the

U.S. Navy, I remember learning about how you could tell if you were on a collision course with another boat. If the other boat does not shift its bearing relative to yours (i.e., does not change its position on your horizon), it means the two of you are going to collide. This figure was not shifting position and was growing ever larger in my field of view.

The figure was that of a woman, taller than most—as tall as me. She was wearing a long flowing white dress and a sheer shawl that flowed in the breeze behind her as she walked. She was an attractive woman, hard to say how old; she moved as if she was on a conveyer belt pulled along by an invisible string—a floating woman. I diverted my eyes, as I did not feel comfortable making eye contact with her. I stopped and she passed by in front of me.

She really got my attention. There was something odd about her, and certainly it was odd to have a woman you don't know approach you with a smile and make direct eye contact with you. I think that is why I looked away. I continued circling the deck, and eventually I stopped aft and leaned against the rail to admire the ocean view. While I was standing there, I noticed the same woman approaching me again. This time I made eye contact. As she drew near me she continued to look into my eyes and smile. The smile was not appropriate for someone who does not know another person. The Pacific Northwest is full of very reserved descendants of Northern European settlers. They tend not to be outgoing, and the custom on ferry crossings is not to flirt on deck but maintain good boundaries.

As the woman passed me, her head turned in my direction, and she made very direct eye contact and smiled like someone admiring an infant in somebody's arms. I watched as she disappeared on the deck. I was struck by her appearance now that we had experienced a closer encounter. Her body and alignment were like a ballet dancer, light of foot and with the head suspended from the sky. But her face was very weathered, like a woman older than her years who had spent a long time living in the Sonora Desert. Her face looked like she could have been 80 or 90—a weird juxtaposition of young body and old face.

We were about halfway in our ferry crossing, and I grew even more curious about this woman. Too bashful and taken aback to say anything during my encounter, I was determined to go find her and ask her who she was and what was going on. I went inside the cabin and made a loop. No floating woman. I went to the next deck; same thing, no floating woman. I repeated my rounds, but this time in the reverse direction. No floating woman. I returned to my car and waited to disembark. While I sat there, I pondered this mysterious encounter. A chilly October evening and here was this woman, lightly clothed in sheer garments walking about on an open deck.

And then a question suddenly struck me. Had I encountered an angel? A living breathing embodied angel? Why me? Then I began to think about how I had spent this day lending a hand to the family. What if my sister Lois' spirit and that of our mother and other loved ones had hovered around us as we helped Ralph with his move? What if this was a way to thank me for my love and concern? I am a very intuitive person and when I returned home, I asked my guides for some clarification. What I received was confirmation—This was an angel. Her name is Terry. Not only was she sent to thank me and connect me with my loving family, she was an angel I could call on whenever I needed her support.

You can believe what you want. I have no proof of this. But as the years pass, I continue to call on Terry for guidance and I am grateful for this connection. I have no other explanation for this lightly clad person who intentionally intersected my path in life. This person who appeared out of nowhere and then disappeared from sight. Before this happened, I imagined angels as only existing in spirit. Now I believe that angels exist in an embodied form as well.

The important question to ask here is what do you believe? I hope this story fuels your curiosity and opens your eyes to the possibility of such an encounter. Let's face it, if it was real and it happened to me, it could happen to you.

—Bruce Hostetter

Victor Street Ghost

I was born in Vancouver, British Columbia, where I lived with my parents and my younger brother for the first eight years of my life. My father worked for a radio station in Vancouver until he was offered a job as a news anchor and program director for KVOS TV in Bellingham, Washington. So in 1953, just after I turned eight, my family moved from Vancouver to a house on Victor Street in the historic Columbia neighborhood of Bellingham.

In early childhood, I would sometimes stare off into space. At first, my mother thought that I was daydreaming, but when it lasted for a long while and I didn't move, she thought maybe I had some form of epilepsy. After many visits to several doctors, nothing was found wrong with me and I was diagnosed as a normal healthy child.

On the day we moved into our new home, I thought that someone was already living there, because as we drove up to the house, I saw an elderly lady with long white hair, wearing a long black dress that tied around her waist, standing under the huge chestnut tree on the small front lawn. When I mentioned to my mother about this lady at our house, she insisted that there was nobody there, and explained to me that it wasn't our house; we were only renting it.

It was an old two-story house built in the 1900s that had an upstairs with two bedrooms and a large walking space under the stairway. Many times I saw the elderly lady in various places in the house, just standing there and watching. Sometimes I would wake up in the morning and she would be standing at the end of my bed; and most times, on our arrival home from somewhere, she would be waiting for us, standing under the chestnut tree.

I remember my dad bringing home our very first television set, a Zenith black and white. Every time we left the room for a few minutes while watching a TV show, it would be turned off when we returned to the room. My dad thought the TV was defective and returned it to the store for a replacement. But the same thing happened with the next one. What my father didn't know was that the elderly lady was standing in front of the TV blocking the picture screen when we came back into the room.

After numerous times of mentioning to my mother about seeing this mysterious elderly lady in the black dress, she began to wonder if maybe I wasn't just imagining things. The next time the real estate lady stopped by to collect our rent, my mother asked her who had lived in the house before us. She responded that her 90-year-old mother had lived there most of her life, and that she had passed away in the house. Quickly, she pulled out a small picture from her wallet and showed it to my mother, who then called me over to look.

With my eyes wide open, I exclaimed, "That's the lady I see in the house!"

The real estate lady was shocked, and needless to say, my mother never doubted me again.

—*Zella Chapman*

Mike's Idea of Heaven

My husband Mike grew up in a commercial fishing family. After two years of college, he quit school to pursue his passion of fishing. He worked in the commercial fishing industry his entire life. It was in his blood. The once-booming industry was in significant decline over the years, and when he was 61, the company where he worked closed its doors. It was overwhelming for him to deal with health issues and the prospect of having to be retrained and begin a whole new career at his age. In the spring of 2003, he took his own life.

I am thankful for a dear friend of mine who was a great help to me when my husband passed away. I had communicated with my mother after her passing, so I was not surprised when this spiritually gifted friend shared her communications with Mike to me.

My children and I enjoyed some nice dinners at my friend's home where she had us all laughing because Mike was right there with us helping her cook the dinner. You see, he loved to cook. He was making suggestions to her as to what to cook for us and how we liked it prepared. One night when she was cooking spaghetti, he offered her some tips on how to do it. He was well known for his spaghetti recipe. Another evening when she was preparing steak for us, he explained to her just how we liked it cooked.

My friend had a collection of chimes hanging in her living room. I happened to comment on how much I liked them. She said, "Oh, I'm so glad you mentioned that because Mike was traveling with me in my car today and he asked me to give you the chime with the angel on it. He said you love chimes and angels. He also said that if he wanted to get your attention, he would ring the chime." This really touched my heart.

There are so many negative things said about what happens to people when they commit suicide. I believe that Mike is in a better place now and he is no longer suffering. I feel his love every day.

On the night of Mike's passing, my daughter had a vivid dream about him. Mike was in Alaska, where he loved to go fishing. The scenery was beautiful. He was at the waterfront and there were fishing boats lined up at the dock as far as the eye could see. Mike was walking in a town where there were many restaurants with people gathered outside. Everyone greeted him warmly, and he enjoyed visiting with the people he met. This dream was Mike's way of communicating with my daughter that he was now in his idea of heaven.

—*Muriel Crusciola*

Chapter 10

Affirmation & Meditation

Everyday Miracles

Healing Grace

"Healing Grace" … I had never heard of this expression before, at least not in my conscious memory, until one morning in January 2016. Living in the Pacific Northwest, that January morning was a typical cold and rainy day, as I rested on the couch with my Peruvian alpaca blanket and tried to sleep after an evening of battling symptoms of an annoying cough/flu. I lay my hand on my chest and as I took some slow deep breaths, I started to think about gratitude, and I just said these words aloud. I think my intention was to heal and restore my body to perfect health through thanking God and the Universe for "Healing Grace," but the impact was much greater. The words invoked the experience of a gentle caress, something like how a warm and gentle breeze feels as it touches your hair and your skin … a comforting and calming experience. It's like that precious moment when a baby reaches his hand up to touch his mother's cheek for the first time—something I experienced with my own son when he was a couple of months new to this world. It's kind of like "slowing it down" and remembering who and what is important.

I count my experience with "Healing Grace" as one of the important moments in my life. At a deeper level, I felt a sense of acceptance or inner knowing that "I am okay" or that "Everything will be okay." It was grounding. I felt hope. I experienced gratitude. "Healing Grace" was—and is—loving.

You might be wondering how this fits with one's life. How is it revealed? For me, it wasn't just a "one off" experience. The answer to how it is revealed or how it fits with one's life is about becoming mindful. It's a process and a practice. It's about taking this expression of "Healing Grace" and integrating it with your own experience, whether that involves coping with daily "hassles" or something far more significant.

Since that January morning, I've made a conscious intention to integrate the practice of saying these words into my daily experience. Like other people, there are times when I feel anxious, a little unsure about something, and maybe struggle or needlessly focus on where I'm stuck. I do indeed recognize and appreciate our humanness. Recently, I was working on a design for a project that involved incorporating some new content. I knew what the expectation was, but I didn't know how to make it fit. I struggled. I would pause and sigh several times. My mind would start to race with thoughts such as, "Get it done" and "Will this work?" At one point, I just stopped what I was doing and focused on saying the words, "Healing Grace." I noticed how my shoulders lowered, my breathing slowed a bit and I started to center myself. I told myself, "I can do this." I experienced a sense of hope. And yes, I did complete the project.

I'm trying to make "Healing Grace" a practice in my life. Sometimes it is easier than other times. I'm learning that we frequently need to first accept "what is" or "what we see and hear" before we can move in directions that offer possibilities or hope.

Sometimes that process is ongoing, especially when we find it hard to accept an event or a decision.

That was certainly my experience this past year when I experienced the adjustments of living apart from my husband of 25+ years. While all logic and planning seemed to lead to the right decision for my husband to take an international work assignment that was extended for 11 months, I needed to shift from a family of four with a somewhat predictable routine of roles and responsibilities and learn to accept that I needed "to do" and "to be" in this world without him under the same roof. That definitely was an ongoing process of acceptance, but one that also created the opportunity for me to figure things out on my own and to strengthen myself. I'm grateful for that learning. I didn't know about "Healing Grace" last year, but it is something I am practicing now since my husband has recently taken another international work assignment. There are moments when I am missing "us." It isn't always easy. Yet, I feel a little more hopeful, a little more centered, and definitely a little more accepting this time around. Sometimes, saying the words "Healing Grace" is enough ... gently bringing me back to the awareness that everything is okay.

I invite you to explore how the expression "Healing Grace" might be helpful to you. Maybe it fits. Maybe it feels like more of a stretch. Maybe it's a nudge for you to choose a different expression, one that is unique, new to you, or simply feels comfortable. The wonderful thing is that we have the freedom to choose whatever works for us. Sometimes that involves trying out something new. Your experience is uniquely yours.

So take this moment to refresh yourself by saying the words, "Healing Grace." Pause before you say these words (out loud or silently in your mind), and simply listen. Notice the silence before you say the words. Notice the silence that falls between each word. Notice the silence in the space after you say them. Simply listen. If it's easier for you, close your beautiful eyes and whisper these words. Notice how saying them makes you feel. Listen to any thoughts that surface in your mind. I invite you to be curious … to have a beginner's mind, and experience the calming beauty of these words.

—Moira Haagen

"My Heart Is Your Heart"

When I was in my early 20s, I experienced a very amazing and powerful guided meditation. This meditation went something like: "Imagine you are walking down a path and down a set of stairs to a door to meet a special guide to give you what you need." I can't remember all the details of the guided imagery. I do, however, remember very well what happened next.

I opened the plain wooden door and saw before me, floating in space, the Sacred Heart of Jesus, in 3-D. This image was familiar to me because I was raised Catholic, and was educated in Catholic schools. Then as the heart image faded, before me appeared a very tall Jesus. He was dressed in off-white robes and had brown hair. I felt the knowing certainty that he was Jesus, the man, but at this moment, he was so tall that his head towered above me, practically in the clouds. I had to crane my neck to try and peer into his face.

I asked him if he could please come down to my size. He immediately did come down to just my size, dressed and looking the same, but exactly my own physical height. He then conveyed to me in words and intense feeling, "My heart is your heart."

This was such an incredibly heartfelt, vivid experience that I have never forgotten it. This meditation was, in some ways, more real and vivid than many "real life" experiences I have had, because it contained DEEP EMOTION, LOVE, vivid detail, and a STRONG, SIMPLE yet VERY POWERFUL MESSAGE. The meaning of it puzzled me for many years, because I wasn't completely sure how my heart could be Jesus's heart. I was conditioned to think that Jesus was God and that Jesus is on a completely different level than I could ever attain.

Now, 30 years later, the meaning of this meditation has become more clear to me. I think that we all have the heart of Jesus, because he was human, just like us, only a very advanced human. We all have the capacity to love others unconditionally, just like Jesus, and we also have the capacity and potentiality to have a strong desire and intention—and even the ability to heal and care for those less fortunate than us, just like Jesus.

This meditation conveyed to me the idea that LOVE is the single most important quality in the world. It also shared the idea that Jesus loves me in a very personal way for who I am, and that I can also love myself. I can potentially love and cherish other people and creatures of our planet unconditionally as well as Jesus does. I can love people through their defense mechanisms, fears, pain, and false trails in life because I know that everyone is doing their best with the information and environment they were raised in. And I can love, cherish, and accept myself, even though I'm not perfect, because I am still dealing with the information and environment in which I was raised.

The Blue Whale's Message

Sometimes I see beautiful visions during meditation. For quite a while, I had been looking for guidance about what to do with my life. Some people told me that they received guidance in meditation, but I never had—not until February 2015, when I was attending a meditation class at Unity. I went into a deep still meditation. A blue whale appeared to me in my meditation. This whale had flyers in his mouth that read, "Save the Whales, Save Earth's Oceans, Help Marine Life." The message was given to me with tremendous spiritual power and strong intent. A message was also conveyed to me that I would receive guidance to do this work.

Afterwards it became clear to me that I have always wanted to save our planet from the pollution and global warming that is threatening to destroy us. I have always been passionate about re-using and recycling and using only non-toxics in my home. I decided I wanted to build rain gardens, as a start. Rain gardens are a way to filter storm water into root systems of plants and render it non-toxic, instead of the heavy metal combo of gas, oil, and pesticides heading to the ocean, via storm drains. A few weeks later I went to a garden store for a few plants. I felt guided (pushed) to ask one person who worked there about rain gardens. She said she teaches people how to build rain gardens. We soon became friends. I decided to attend her class.

A week later another friend texted me about a clean water presentation at the RE Store in Bellingham. I met a woman there who is one the North Sound Bay Keepers. She is passionate about finding ways to keep polluted storm water from reaching the Bay. She said that car brake pads are made with copper. Small amounts of copper rub off when we brake. This inevitably ends up in storm water drains. Even micro amounts of copper are very bad for fish, especially salmon. It causes them to lose their navigation system. In fact, cars are the biggest culprit for global warming and pollution reaching the oceans. People can ride their bikes, walk, or take public transit, instead of driving. I am going to do that much more. I told her I would become one of her storm water stewards. She invited me to go on a tour of our city's storm water system. She also said she would love to give her presentation at my neighborhood association's next meeting. My friend from the garden store also wants to talk at this meeting.

—Polly Richter

My Secret for Instant Bliss

O nce upon a time, I decided to get rich selling residential real estate. Sure, I'd flopped in a few previous career choices, but this was going to be different. Yeah, right! Unfortunately, my sales numbers were pathetic and thinking back on it, understandably so. I just didn't fit the profile you think of when describing a successful sales person. I was extremely shy, overweight, depressed, and to make things worse, suffered from stage-fright and something called "sales-call reluctance." I could dream up every excuse in the book to not approach a sales prospect, especially a "for-sale-by owner," which at the time was the bread and butter for most Realtors. But fortunately, while on the verge of throwing in the towel, I got either very lucky or, depending on your point of view, received a miracle.

One evening, I was rehearsing a "listing (sales) presentation" while alone in my real estate office. I was speaking out loud while smiling broadly and looking into a mirror of sorts, created by the interior office lights reflecting off the large plate-glass windows. This practice speech was designed to be positive, mood elevating, and motivational. It was to be given in hopes of persuading the homeowner to "list" their home with myself and my company.

After perhaps 40 or 50 minutes of "huffing and puffing" into this mirror, I started to notice some changes in how I was feeling and acting. I was beginning to speak more forcefully. My voice seemed to be projecting better, and wasn't "cracking" like it frequently did when I was nervous. My gestures seemed to be more natural, more animated. My eye contact felt a lot better, and I was actually beginning to enjoy looking at myself in the mirror for a change. My smile seemed more spontaneous, less artificial. I was starting to feel like smiling instead of having to fake it.

At the same time I was feeling more cheerful, relaxed, confident, and optimistic. And I was starting to get excited. I thought to myself, Wow, maybe I really can become a better salesman. Maybe I've accidently found a way to miraculously change from being an introvert to an extrovert in one hour. Maybe a person's "self-image" can be changed more easily than I thought. Just get in front of a mirror, start smiling, and speak positively and out loud. And start to envision success.

Think back for a moment, if you will, to where I was coming from—a place of weakness, and all of a sudden, I've gone from hopeless failure to super-salesman. What was happening to me? Why was I feeling and acting so differently? I was experiencing what people refer to today as "runner's high" or "stage-performer's high."

So, to make a long story short, I did start listing more homes for sale after that evening's experience. I used this new knowledge to elevate my self-confidence prior to listing appointments. I did become a better sales person using this new knowledge and skill.

But of course nowadays this is nothing new. Many of us are aware of the ability to elevate mood and confidence by "pumping ourselves up" by and speaking out loud while looking into a mirror and smiling. But this was over 40 years ago; success coaching was not common then, and it was definitely a breakthrough experience for me.

So, as I say, things got better but then, quite some time later, I made another accidental discovery that eventually led to something even more significant and much more miraculous in my view. I noticed that sometimes during my mood elevating sessions, I would experience an occasional episode of "frisson." I'm referring to the extremely pleasurable physical response, commonly referred to as " cold chills" and usually accompanied by goosebumps. And, most important, when I experienced one or more episodes of frisson during practice speech, I would reach my goal of the "runners natural high," the confident, upbeat mood, etc., much more quickly. The goosebumps experience was so powerful and pleasurable it would frequently and almost instantly lead to an elevated positive mood.

So, I started thinking, if I could create one or more episodes of frisson at will, I could cut down on the amount of time it took me to elevate my mood, to get "pumped up." And sure enough, quite by accident again, I had a flash of insight and learned the amazing skill of how to evoke frisson at will. And not just one episode; I could string several of these "mood elevating" episodes of frisson together for an even more dramatic, more powerful, and longer lasting "runners/public-speakers high."

Years later, I learned why frisson episodes can be so powerful. Scientific studies have shown that frisson is associated with elevated levels of the neurotransmitter dopamine, the body's natural mood booster.

—*Neal Engelking*

Nightly Affirmation

I am now speaking to my Heavenly Father, Great Spirit, and Source Energy.

I am now speaking to my spirit guides and the master Guide Spirit.

I am now speaking to my Guardian Angels who are always surrounding me.

I am now speaking to the Arch Angels and especially to Michael and Rafael.

I am now speaking to every former family member, friend, and others my life may have touched who are now residing in the Spiritual Plane.

I am now speaking to every other one currently residing in the Spiritual Plane who watches over and guides me, insuring that I am always moving forward on my own personal path to achieving and receiving my highest good.

To all of these I say "Thank you" (five times) for every blessing, gift, and treasure that has manifested in my life to this point.

"Thank you" (five times) for every blessing, gift, and treasure that is already in route to me and not yet revealed.

"Thank you"(five times) for every blessing, gift, and treasure that you holding for me, knowing better than me the perfect time for those manifestations.

"Thank you" (five times) for providing me with the perfect health and endless wealth that allows me the resources to serve YOU by serving others.

—Jon Strong

Chapter 11

Many Paths to Unity

Everyday Miracles

Remembering Who I Am

As a child I was very shy. I was afraid of everything and everybody in general. My mother was overprotective and instilled that fear in me. I have tried not to instill this fear in my own daughter, though I have not always been successful in that regard. But wait, I am getting ahead of myself ... My father was a wonderful but quiet man who didn't know how to express himself emotionally. I had one brother, six years older, and we were not close as children. To him, I was merely a pest. He called me "Maggie" just to give me a bad time. Although I didn't have any sisters, my younger cousin was like a sister to me. To this day, we are very close friends. In the first grade, I met a girl who watched over me like a mother hen. When she moved away in the fourth grade, I was devastated.

My communication with others during those early years was strained, to say the least. I never knew what to say or do most of the time. So, I was left out of most activities and never felt like I belonged anywhere. School was not a joy to me. During those troubled times, I was literally alone most of the time. I remember one day, in particular, when I was lying on the lawn in front of our house looking up into the sky. I must have been around nine years old at the time. I wondered if "God" was up there in the sky.

I really longed for that connection. I had felt this longing even at a younger age when I strained to make contact with God.

Later in my teenage years, I came across a pamphlet written by Norman Vincent Peale about positive thinking. I was astounded and couldn't get enough of this information. I had never seen or read anything like it before. It awakened a longing in me, a recognizing of something deep within myself that I had never experienced in my life. I know now that it was really a remembering and reawakening of my soul.

This experience must have stayed with me, even though I didn't think much more about it for quite awhile. I went on to community college to take up secretarial skills, as my mother thought I needed to get a good "office job" and get married. I found a job in the insurance claims adjusting field. I moved to Seattle, where I continued to work in the insurance field, and met the love of my life. We met at the Methodist Church at a singles group. He liked to attend the Gregorian Chants at the Episcopalian Church. When I went to hear the chants, a wonderful feeling came over me, a deep knowing and yearning, just as I had felt as a child. Sadly, our romance ended that same year, and I was completely devastated.

At the Methodist Church group I soon met my future husband and married him on the rebound, which was a grave mistake. However, I did get one beautiful, joyous thing from the union with my husband—a daughter, whom I love dearly. So there is good that comes from everything. When she was first born and the nurse laid her next to me, her eyes were wide open. Looking into my daughter's eyes, it seemed as if I was looking into eternity! It was a wonderful feeling, beyond anything I had ever before experienced.

My husband and I moved to Los Angeles, literally to escape from his mother. She had mental problems and created havoc wherever she went. Then she moved to Los Angeles, too! While living in LA, I worked for an insurance company. One day during my lunch hour, I took a walk downtown and came across the Religious Science Church. It was huge, taking up a whole city block. As I walked around the church, it started to pull me in. Every time I got close to going inside, I lost my nerve and walked away. One afternoon, I finally made it as far as the office door but escaped again. The next day, I went inside the door. There was a woman sitting at a desk and when I said I wanted to talk to someone, she directed me to a chaplain of sorts. This woman didn't really encourage me, but I poured out my heart to her anyway, telling her all about my marital problems. There were a lot of them! All she said in response to my troubles was that she would pray for me, and I wondered, Is that all there is to this?

Sadly, this church couldn't save my marriage. But it saved my life. After my divorce, I moved to Bellingham with my daughter. I returned to college to get a degree in Medical Assisting and found a job as a medical transcriptionist. There was a new Unity Church starting in Bellingham, and I became one of the early members. That is where I found my spiritual home.

During that time, I also studied spiritualism and became a reverend in the Universal Church of the Master. I studied under Reverend Dollie Sanders who, at that time, was a well-known psychic in the area. I attended her meditation group and, while there, I learned to channel spirits. Channeling to me was like an energy and thought pattern that came in through the back of my head and out my mouth. It was easy and effortless. Among other spirits,

I channeled a higher spirit known only as John. I ended up giving a few lectures, and I also gave readings. When Dollie moved away, I started a church of my own. Sometime during that same period in my life, I went to a café to have coffee. As I sat down at a table, I distinctly heard a male voice in my inner ear saying, "I AM THE CHRIST"! This was very enlightening to me to say the least!

Now, I have the privilege of being a chaplain at the Unity Spiritual Center in Bellingham, and I am thankful to learn under Brother Bob Trask.

—*Alita Walton*

The Impossible Takes
a Little Longer

Teddy was the youngest of five children. His father, a Unitarian minister, committed suicide when Teddy was only four years old. His mother, an aspiring Kansas City actress, always longed to appear on the Broadway stage. And so the play began in 1915 when Reverend Jones took his own life and his wife Mary Vern gathered up her young brood of four boys and one girl and began the long trip across the country to New York City.

Mary Vern taught the children how to sing and dance, how to perform in theatrical skits, and how to recite entertaining stories and poems. They stopped at each small town along the way to New York and appeared in local vaudeville houses to earn enough money to continue following their dream eastward.

When they finally arrived in New York one year later, they all crammed into a small, cold water flat on East 42nd Street and everyone journeyed out to daily auditions until they were all employed in small roles on Broadway.

Now Teddy, being the youngest and smallest in the family, was given a very specific chore. Whenever the family was unable to pay their bills or needed food or couldn't gather up enough money to pay the rent, it was his job to deliver this unfortunate news to the landlord or grocer and ask for help. Being a good little actor and relishing his special task of helping his mother, brothers, and sister to survive, he happily overcame any hesitation or fears and performed his duties with much enthusiasm and delight.

Years passed and Teddy grew up, eventually getting a job at WCRB radio station in Boston. At first he just performed minor duties, then advanced to presenting the weather and short news reports. Next came his own disc jockey show ... sales rep ... management ... vice president of the company ... president ... and eventually, he bought the station, turning it into the only classical radio station in the Boston area.

So Teddy became very successful—a multi-millionaire, but he stepped aside as president at the age of 65 to attain a college degree from Boston University and fulfill his life's dream of becoming a Unitarian minister like his dad by graduating from Harvard Divinity School at age 72. He went on to preach for the next sixteen years until his death in 1991.

When I first met Ted Jones in 1974, he shared the secret of his success with me. "I'm not the smartest man in the room," he said. "But most people try to avoid problems and shy away from confrontation. Because I was the youngest and smallest in our family, I was taught from an early age to be the one to show up whenever things got rough and ask for help. All my life I've looked for problems to solve and was the first one to show up whenever something was going wrong. I'd then look to find others who were much smarter than me and asked for help in solving it. As they gathered around to figure out what to do, I'd step back to encourage and support everyone until we all came to a satisfactory solution. I could always get things done without being concerned who took the credit."

Yes, it all began years ago when little Teddy was expected to be the one who fearlessly showed up whenever there was something unpleasant or difficult to be worked out and ask for help. For many years, I was fortunate to call this man my father-in-law, my mentor, and my friend. On his desk was a small engraved gold plaque with the motto:

The difficult we do right away.

The impossible takes a little bit longer.

—Jonathan Hall

Experiencing Unity

In the fall of 2007, I was looking for a spiritual community in Bellingham, Washington. I tried out several different churches, and then decided on Unity of Bellingham. I enjoyed the fun atmosphere at Unity where people accepted and loved each other. I felt more at home there because of the kindness of others, and the size of this spiritual center was just right.

During the years that I have attended Unity, we have had three different ministers. Each minister brought a different style and presence. In the early days with Pete Rhea as the minister, I felt a welcoming presence that made me want to stay at Unity. Reverend Rhea gave talks that were interesting and enlightening. The plays, directed by Kathy Murray, were fun to watch and be a part of. We also have had many talent shows since I came into the scene in 2007.

After many years of service as a fine minister, Pete Rhea was ready to retire at the end of 2009. We had a special service for him in December of that year in which he took questions from the congregation and it was fun for everyone. Pete then retired as our minister.

The new minister that followed in January of 2010 was Reverend Lennis Baugh. He had a wonderful attitude at the beginning of his tenure as minister. His energy helped the church grow, with more families coming in than before. His charisma was evident, and he gave some fine talks that had good truth in them.

After Reverend Baugh left the spiritual center, we went through a transition period where we were in search of a minister for twenty months. Sally Ledgerwood, our church administrator, made a big difference by bringing in some great guest speakers during this transition. Bob Trask was one of those guest speakers, and he eventually became our new minister in June of 2014. Bob Trask has been a speaker on spiritual issues for many years. He is well rounded and has a strong presence here at Unity. I believe that his talks are passionate, truthful, and well received. We are fortunate to have him here at Unity.

Brother Bob recognizes others who have made a difference at the Spiritual Center. One of those people is Kathy Murray, our former music director. I have performed in talent shows at the church throughout the years, but was hesitant about joining the choir. I decided to join the choir members in the fall of 2014. It has been a fun and meaningful experience overall. I have made friends with choir members, and the experience of singing with them has changed me for the better. Kathy Murray is the best music director that I know of. We were fortunate to have her as our director for the past 32 years.

The whole experience at Unity has been heartfelt and well worth the time spent there. There have been times when I really needed spiritual support, and I have always found it. Hallelujah! I am grateful for my home church, Unity of Bellingham.

—*Aaron Buhler*

Finding My Way Back Home

From the time I was a young child, the desire to know "God" was quite strong in me. My paternal family's roots are in the Baptist religion and my maternal family was non-denominational; yet all were part of the fundamental Christian teachings. The judgments, criticism, and attitudes of these religions created a feeling of sadness in me that I did not like. When I reached the age of 20, my first introduction to Jehovah's Witnesses came into play. I really thought they were the chosen ones and knew everything there was to know about the Bible and "Christian" living. This persuasion was strong enough to keep me hooked for about 25 years, after marrying a man of the same religion.

Partly due to the security of my marriage, I didn't question these values. Having three children and working at a regular job kept my days too full to question anything, much less do any research. I didn't even know where to begin. Critical thinking was certainly a void in my upbringing; keeping quiet was the only way to be safe and unharmed. Even though my intuition gave me plenty of messages that this way of life was not feeding my highest good, I did not know how to listen to this evidence of what was "really" true for me at that time. My thoughts were that others knew more than I did; yet my heart yearned for a happiness and freedom that I couldn't find in this belief system.

Once my children were old enough to begin their quest for their own truth, many questions arose with the horrifying exposure of child sexual abuse experienced by my daughter's friend. I learned of incidents in other families as well, but it was all being hushed and no one in the religious community was held accountable. That is a very long story in itself, but it was the final turning point for me to sever all ties to the Watchtower Organization at about age 45, even though I had realized several years before that time that I wanted out. This process was not easy, because I would be leaving all the people who had been a part of my "tribe," literally putting myself in a position of having to start my life over, walking away to never look back. I contemplated the thought, Where will I go and what will I do? Or better yet, Who will I BE?

During this time my daughter had been invited to attend a Unity service in north Spokane. (We lived in Spokane for 27 years.) She was quite impressed with the message and the people. I decided to attend on another occasion and was equally touched, moved, and inspired by the message. After continuing to attend, my heart was opened on a level I had never felt before; the connection to Spirit was deeper and higher than I knew was possible.

Once I made the choice to leave my marriage, a whole new world opened to me. There was a class at Unity for those who wanted to be platform assistants, and after completing the course I knew this was my HOME. I felt as though I was walking above the ground. My joy and happiness were reconnected with ME. The wisdom gained has been a treasure, giving me a sense of joy and freedom beyond anything I had ever experienced.

My depth of gratitude, along with a yearning for learning, continues daily. A personal development course at Landmark Education allowed me to experience a breakthrough in which I recognized my desire to work with children and facilitate inspiring and fun programs. Realizing what children go through in their quest for truth and belonging, I started helping out with the youth groups to experience what Unity offers to children of all ages. The various camps Unity has designed for children from ages 7-18, arranged by age groups; the teacher workshop held every January; and all the support within the congregation has been an inspiring experience for me.

At one point, when the opportunity was presented to facilitate the youth program, I accepted the position and went on to help many children attend camps and other outings. I have seen young people flourish from the personal interaction and the information received through the Unity Youth Program Curriculum and Camps. Seeing young ones grow and mature, free from the guilt, shame, and judgment I experienced through many religious organizations, is inspiring and touches my heart deeply.

My life has been forever blessed, and my horizons of awareness, spiritual growth, and connectedness have reached a higher level of consciousness by being an integral part of the Unity experience at a pivotal time in my life.

—RoseMarie Longmire

The Deeps that You Cannot See

My very first piece of mail was sent to me by my grandmother, a little comicbook-sized pamphlet called *WEE WISDOM*. I remember it well. We had just moved to a new home, I was in a new school starting the third grade, and everything was new and different.

My mom had been an English teacher in her younger years, and was very concerned that I was behind in reading. She must have shared those concerns with my grandmother, because when I arrived home from school that September afternoon, she announced that there was mail that had just been sent to me.

The articles and pictures were printed on grade Z paper with wood chunks left in it, and the pictures were black and white and orange. Not very interesting to an eight year old, but it was my very own magazine, and I dragged it around with me everywhere. Over the years, it grew to be a favorite as I began to comprehend more of the articles and affirmations. It fit with the *Daily Word* (also sent by my grandmother), which was read and discussed over breakfast each morning. The reading of "The Word" each morning and prayers at meals continued while I lived at home through high school and college.

As much as mail had become a joy to look forward to while

serving in Vietnam, I never subscribed to the *Daily Word*. Now I realize that this mental mistake almost led to my demise. Without the spiritual guidance and loving shelter of the Word, I would be left in doubt and fear for several years, until I moved to a sleepy little town called Bellingham, on the North Puget Sound in Washington. I found a job tying fishing net on the docks of Bellingham Bay.

While driving home from work one evening, I noticed a little building on "D" street with a sign on it that said UNITY. I determined to attend the following Sunday and check it out.

When I arrived at the church, the place was about half full. I sat in the back hoping not to be noticed. Thankfully, no one asked me to stand up and introduce myself. At that time it would have been terrifying to be called out of hiding. I just wanted to find out what this congregation believed and how they interpreted the Bible. I had been reading various versions since high school, but I could not get out of them the love that was supposedly there. I read a lot of gloom and doom, of purgatory and laws that seemed anything but loving.

The service began with a very kind, elderly gentleman reading the *Daily Word*. I don't remember the subject that day, but I do remember that for the first time in a long time, I believed there was a God of love somewhere, and these people obviously believed that, too. As I was leaving the church that morning, I had to walk past the minister at the door. He reached out and shook my hand and then pulled me into a hug. Being a macho kind of guy, I was not used to hugs from men, but somehow from Pastor Eddy, it seemed real, and I wanted to experience more of what this group was doing.

It was 1976. I began a new subscription to *Daily Word* and

began a path of discovery and growth that continues to this day. Over the years, I would watch this little church go through many iterations and pastors and speakers. I watched the congregation grow in size and build a new church across town. By 1980, I had been there long enough to be involved in the administration of the church and became a member of the board. I was always hoping for something that would spark the church and the pastor to teach the deeper meanings of the Bible. However, all the talks and sermons were aimed at not offending the congregants. In other words, what was being taught was the "sincere milk of the word" and I wanted the meat. What is God really saying? What am I to understand about the teaching?

In the mid-1980s, we were preparing for a new Unity minister, and I was in hope of someone that would really knock our socks off with spiritual knowledge. The day he arrived was a Tuesday, and I wanted to meet him, so drove over to the church to introduce myself. He was coming out of the back door as I walked up to the church from the parking lot. He was wearing a nice suit and looked pretty slick, but when he put on his dark glasses before shaking my hand, I thought to myself that this guy was not the one to teach love to the people. I knew I would have to make a special effort if I was going to get through his seemingly standoffish manner.

Over the years, I did make a little progress with Pastor Rhey, but only after I understood his background and training. He was bashful. He had a lot of knowledge, but did not want to expose himself to the deeper kinds of love that Unity was founded upon. His teaching was flowery on the surface, but powerful if studied in depth, so I would tape his talks and listen to them during the week. Some were very helpful for deepening my understanding. Others were a shoulder shrug, but all were spoken with the sincerity of someone who had grown up in the Unity family.

Pete and I became friends and we went to lunch sometimes, and I even took him and his wife Terrisa sailing. When the Unity poet laureate James Dillit Freeman came to visit Bellingham, I was able to take Pete, Terry, and Jim sailing. This was a thrill for me, because I had admired J. D. Freeman's poetry since the third grade. Now here he was with me on my boat.

As we sailed off on a beautiful sunset cruise, Freeman looked out over the bay and remarked, "You know, there are deeps out there that you cannot see. So it is with people." Those words have stuck with me ever since, and have helped me to withhold judgment about people and their actions.

In 1986, a different kind of speaker came and gave a talk that proved to me that there were deeper ways than we were being taught, and that there were things to understand and use in life to make positive and loving relationships with people and my Creator. I bought his book God's Phone Number and asked him to sign it. It changed my life!

A few years later, I left Unity church after Pete left. The transitional speakers seemed to be a series of wing nuts without Biblical interest or understanding. At that time, I began to pray diligently for teachers and revelation knowledge that would help me understand who I am, what I am, where I am, how I got here, and what am I supposed to be doing about it. The Lord answered my prayers in a flood of Biblical teaching.

After visiting a few churches in north Whatcom County, I found a pastor who was a Greek scholar who had just been kicked out of the largest church in Lynden for teaching that the resurrection had already taken place, and Jesus was alive and had actually "come again!" The Lord led me to study with this man. When I visited him at his home and noticed a copy of the Metaphysical Bible Dictionary by Charles Fillmore in his library, I knew I was home. Finally, here was a spiritual teacher I could relate to.

During the years away from Unity, I would visit the church and wonder why people there would not want to have someone with revelation knowledge teach the deeper meanings that were authored by its founders. The meanings and attributes of God's Words held the key (for me) to see the stories and battles and parables of the Bible as a personal mirror, designed to meet my needs and help me understand all people and situations. When that church broke up and the pastor went to get his Doctorate in Theology at St. Andrews in Scotland, I was without a church for a while. Then I read in the paper that the speaker who had impressed me so many years ago was going to speak again at Unity in Bellingham, and I went to hear him. When I found out that he was the new minister, I was shocked. I thought, "Man, what are you doing here in this church when you could be teaching anywhere you want? And, how will the church pay for such an excellent speaker?" However, I have learned not to question the actions of my Heavenly Father, but to assist the energy in whatever way I can.

True Unity is a rich and vast treasure chest that opens only to those who look for it within themselves. Christ in you, the hope of Glory!

—George Rounthwaite

Chapter 12

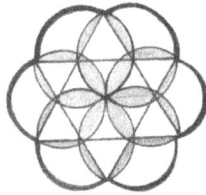

Miracle Workers

Everyday Miracles

My Mom, the Healer

Many years ago, I visited my dear Uncle Mel and found him in a wheelchair. This surprised and saddened me because he had always been so athletic, and since he sold his chicken farm ten years earlier had become almost a fanatic golfer. But his arthritis and diabetes had crippled him and it was painful to see this active, outgoing man being an invalid. Even moving his arms caused him pain.

And yet it was not only his physical self that had suffered, for his wonderful, laughing personality had also dimmed; he either grumbled or sat silent, tucked inside himself, a bear in hibernation. Two days of this and I was also becoming despondent; it seemed the whole house was sinking into a cold darkness. If he was dying, I could more easily have tolerated his gloom, but he was not dying.

So, as I have done so many times, I turned to my mom, who, since her death, had been ready to help those in need. In the dimension she now occupies, she is as close to me as my skin, and when I direct my healing intention through her, she never refuses me. But I must be confident of her help, assured that my prayer will be answered. I cannot come to her pleading, waffling, hoping she will help; I must be confident and clear of the outcome.

Isn't it true that we are physically made of energy and its vibrations? And aren't the energies of healing stronger than the energies of illness? Surely that is so; otherwise none of us would live past childhood. Mom has that healing energy (also called Grace) available whenever we need it. I have experienced its results so many times that I now know I can count on it.

One afternoon I saw Uncle Mel in his wheelchair half asleep and I moved quietly behind him. Quietly, because I did not want him to see what I was doing and have his self-doubts impede the flow of Grace.

I held my open hands over his head until I felt a heat radiating from them, meanwhile imagining the light of Grace pouring from Mom, through me, into him and affirming:

"Mama, I know you are with me, and we're now getting Uncle Mel out of this wheelchair and back into enjoying his life. Your healing love is pouring through me and we're making him well." After about five minutes, I let my hands fall to my sides and moved away. He remained dozing, with his head down. I doubt he even knew I was standing there behind him, loving him.

The next day I flew back to my home in Oregon. When I walked in the door the phone was ringing; it was Aunt Eva telling me through tears that Uncle Mel was up and walking and nearly pain free. I was filled with appreciation and laughing with joy. I didn't tell her though, that it was Mom who had healed him; I thought she would have found that a bit far-fetched.

For weeks Uncle Mel lived again the life he had always loved, and was even back on the golf course. But then, a month or so later, he returned to his wheelchair and, this time, he would not escape it before he died.

I had learned a valuable lesson. Uncle Mel needed his suffering more than he needed his joy, and only he could change that. I knew him well, knew that there were things for which he felt no forgiveness, and that there were those who hurt him whom he refused to forgive. Somehow his suffering provided a balance for his unresolved guilt and resentment and his wheelchair became the cross to which he nailed himself.

Uncle Mel was not a victim, but a creator. To see him as a victim would unfairly minimize the powerful man that he was. He was a creator and his attitude was the director of his creations. Neither I, nor my mom, had the right or the ability to take away Uncle Mel's freedom to live and die as he chose.

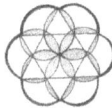

Years later a small Canadian boy named Jimmy was stricken by a cancerous growth in his brain. His doctors said his type of cancer was more than 90% fatal no matter what treatments were employed. Still, they did their best. Yet after more than a year of radiation and chemotherapy, they gave up and sent Jimmy home to die.

When I learned of this I again called upon Mom and insisted that this little boy be cured and allowed to grow up and become the man of his dreams. That was ten years ago; Jimmy is now in high school, playing sports, and having a normal boyhood.

Thanks Mom.

—Bob Trask

With These Hands

From the time I was a child, I recall being able to sense a force or pressure with my hands around plants, animals, trees, and people. At the time, I did not know what it was. As I reached my late twenties, moments happened that encouraged me to want to know more about what these different sensations meant. I asked others if they could feel an emanation around things similar to what I experienced, and many could not. This opened a doorway to the spiritual path I embarked upon and the mysterious happenings that began to occur in my life.

For several weeks a month, I studied with Guru Dev in southern Oregon at the Foundation for Meditative Studies. At that time, I was studying Absuchanka, an ancient chakra/emotional healing modality. Two years later, we left the ashram, taking what we had learned and the wisdom garnered into our working lives. From there, a dear friend suggested that I research Reiki to learn how to share the "sensing instrument" in my hands. I then attuned through the process to become a Reiki master. Following my friend's guidance, I then embarked on the path to becoming a Universal Brotherhood minister to offer healing guidance to others.

After setting up several rooms in my home—a fully equipped

hair salon, esthetic room, meditation room, and healing room, I offered Chakra Balancing and meditation, and taught clients how to access their inner intelligence to recover answers to conditions or problems they were experiencing.

The adventure into the healing realm began with my own personal healing by recalling past lives, cellular memories, emotional imprints, and various other self-realization practices. I spent several years studying the healing practices of the Native American shaman and the Tibetan Buddhist Lama Rimpoche. I learned about garden flower essences through the work of Michelle Small Wright and created a Perelandra garden (to discover the world beyond sight that maintains the Earth). I also studied Bassett aromatherapy and massage therapy, eventually completing an eight-year Naturopathy program, and became a hypnotherapist. My curiosity also carried me into the healing practices contained within the I AM teachings, meditative practices in the Buddhist teachings, Christian healing delving into the healing powers of Jesus, and chanting the Vedic sounds of life. As I followed my intuition, I was led down a path to explore who I Am and to discover the magnificent realms of consciousness that we live within and that we can learn to access for the purposes of healing.

As I assisted others in their healing, more doors opened into the profound mysteries of healing. Twenty-five years ago, I was a professional cosmetologist, offering hair design, esthetics, and practicing energy healing. During that time, I experienced three miraculous healings that were instantaneous. Each time, the healing occurred in the moment without my conscious awareness or intention. All I offered was guidance, allowing the powers of healing to flow and sustaining a focused presence with my clients.

Here are stories of those experiences in which I witnessed instantaneous healings.

Jess and Lya

Working in the salon at the time, I was cutting the hair of a young male client who was just graduating from college. Jess emanated a sadness or concerned state as he sat in the chair and we talked. I mentioned to him that I could sense the state he was in. At that moment, an energy radiated from his chest and raised the cape, knocking the scissors out of my hand, which then hit the wall. Stunned, we both stared at each other as we regained our composure. I asked him what he was feeling in his heart. I asked if I could place my hands over his heart and he replied "yes." I could feel a hot prickly sparking sensation in my hands. I asked him if he would like to share what he was feeling.

He began to share with me the mixed feelings he had about his long-time girlfriend Lya, who wanted to get married after college graduation. He explained that he had been in school since he was five years old and wanted to travel and explore life for a while before embarking on the course of marriage. Jess expressed a fear that Lya may not want to wait a few more years or may find someone else. Jess clearly loved her and wanted to marry her, just not at that time. I allowed Jess the space to share all his thoughts and feelings. I asked him to close his eyes and place his awareness in the area of his heart. I then asked him to identify the feeling in his heart. In an instant, he realized that it was courage he needed to have the conversation with Lya. And he understood that he would have to trust that what he wanted was as valuable as her desire to get married. He wanted to be honest with her and not have any regrets later on. The sensation in my hands disappeared and the area around Jess's heart felt peaceful. I finished cutting his hair, he thanked me, and left the salon.

Jordan

In the late summer, working from home, I had a long-time male client that I had not seen for a couple months. As the thought of Jordan entered my mind, I picked up the phone to call him. Jordan was a tall man with a strong stature who expressed firm independent nature. He owned a large construction company and was very successful. When Jordan answered my call, he said he was happy to hear that I was thinking of him. He went on to say he'd had an accident that injured his spine, and he was unable to move and had been lying flat on his back for two months. Jordan's voice was humble and trembled as he shared his story. He shared with me that a nurse had been with him twenty-four hours a day helping with all his needs, including helping him to use a bed pan.

As I listened to his voice, I imagined him standing in front of me. I moved my hand over his heart area, and asked him to close his eyes and take a deep breath, and then release it. I asked him where he felt the pain in his spine while guiding him to bring his awareness to that area. I then asked Jordan to take another deep breath and move that breath from his lower spine up to his heart and release the pain with his breath through his heart. I moved my hand over his body as if we were in the same room, even though he was in his bed and I at home. I guided him through this process several times, continuing to ask him if he had any other feelings bothering him or pain anywhere. He mentioned the feeling of helplessness in his body, and the gratitude to his nurse for helping him through his healing process. Each time I asked a question, he shared what he felt and followed my guidance. Then there was an instant when he broke the silence to ask me, "What are you doing?" I shared with him that I was moving my hand in the same direction I was guiding him as if I were right there with him. I then asked Jordan why he asked. He said, "I can move my legs and the pain is gone!"

Stunned by this experience, we were both speechless. I couldn't explain to him or myself "why it happened." We only knew that he was able to move his legs with no pain. I had trusted my intuition to allow my hands to guide his healing. In that moment there was no separation between us and he was healed.

Connie

Connie, then in her seventies, was a clients who came in to get her hair done one morning. She shared with me that she was scheduled to have knee surgery and she was not looking forward to it. The doctor had taken an x-ray showing her where the problem was. I asked her if she would want to understand why her knee was bothering her. She did not understand the question and I explained that there could be a cellular memory involved, an earlier incident, as a young child perhaps, that may be stuck in her knee. She mentioned that no one had ever said that before and that she was a bit skeptical, but she went along with it. I placed my hands over her knee. She explained that she had a fear of the water since childhood. Without apprehension, Connie said she would like to know if this could be a possibility.

I asked Connie to close her eyes and breathe deeply to get very relaxed. I then guided her awareness to her knee and instructed her to ask her knee if it had a memory causing the pain. She envisioned herself as about five years old standing on the ocean shore. As the waves washed in an out between her legs, she got buried in the sand and she was stuck, unable to move. When the waves rose above her knees, she screamed in a panic, thinking she was in great danger. Her mother heard her cries and immediately helped her out of the water.

When Connie discovered her fear of water, she realized that she had screamed to be saved. In that moment, I asked her to take a deep breath and led her back to a state of presence. She sat silently for a bit, and then shared her experience. Connie was amazed that she had recalled this memory so vividly. As she stood up, she realized that the pain in her knee was gone. I suggested that her doctor take another x-ray before the planned surgery. The x-ray came back normal with no surgery needed.

Today, I know it is not me doing anything that makes healing happen, but rather allowing my intuition, presence, and focus of the unified field, the universal life-force energy, to tend to the situation at hand. The unified field of energy and light flows through us, and by trusting our intuition, it helps us through the process of discovering what we want to be, do, have or feel, realizing that by allowing the flow we can help one another to feel whole.

—*Christina Lorraine*

Birth Family
The Inner Library

Years ago, when I had a private hypnotherapy practice in south Seattle, I had a client in her early 30s that I will call "Betty." She had a very hard life and was calling for help. She presented as bi-polar with rapid shifting from depression to mania. She also sought out dangerous situations and activities when she was in a manic state, including prostitution. This was at the time when the "Green River killer" was in the Seattle area, and Betty had a bad experience that scared her enough to seek help.

I always prayed and sent healing energy to all of my clients. With Betty, I used a hypnotherapy technique that involved an inner library where all her negative emotions and unresolved issues were on the left side of her library, and everything that was right in her life was on the right side. By the time we had worked through most of her negative emotions, her mood swings were almost gone and some unresolved issues began coming to the surface.

She became aware of a pain caused by her belief that her parents never wanted her and had not given her any love. I used a common hypnotherapy technique that took her back to her feelings about being born into her family when she was in the womb. Betty became extremely emotional and started crying, "Stop fighting, stop fighting!" Not really knowing what to do, I reacted by telling her to take a couple of deep breaths, relax, and go back further in time to when she first knew she was to be born into this family.

As she took the breaths, I saw her whole body relax. I also was praying for help because I had not been in a situation like this before. My next suggestions were similar to suggestions used in past life regression. I suggested that she trust God, or her higher power and the part of her that knows, as she goes back to when she first knew she would be born into this family.

When her facial expression indicated that she was in peace and ready to share her current experience, I asked Betty if she was indoors or out, alone or with someone. Betty reported that she was with a kind man in a long robe. She said they were walking on the grass and he was telling her it was not a good idea for her to go to that family, but she was arguing with him and insisting that she had so much love to give them and they were so unhappy; she knew them and loved them, and therefore she needed to go to them. She was so insistent that he finally agreed, but warned her that it was not going to be easy and she may regret it. She reported that she was feeling so much love in that place. I suggested that she absorb all the love she could in that place, and to let it heal her pain and anything else that was appropriate for her before returning to normal consciousness and moving on with the rest of her day. I asked her to share her experience with me, and made an appointment with her for a few days later.

When Betty came in for her next appointment, she was beautiful and appeared to be quite peaceful. Betty said she had never been so happy. She went into her inner library again and found that everything was on the right side of her library. She said there were a few shelves on the left side, but they were empty. She kept in contact with me for the next couple of years until I left the area. She got a job, a loving relationship, and had no more depression or manic episodes.

I started using this technique with other clients. It always brought healing and noticeable change to their lives. I believe they were healed because they were able to see that they are not victims but chose this life for a purpose, including the experiences they must have to fulfill their purpose. I never encountered anyone who had not agreed to being born in this life and to the family situation they were born into.

—*Emma Jones*

Listening to the Body's Wisdom

This year I celebrated my 76th birthday. I am retired after teaching physics and computer science to college students for thirty years. Life is fun these days. My wife Elly and I enjoy walking in our neighborhood, preparing healthy food, and feel grateful for our life together. Staying healthy is our top priority. I like to keep my body in tune by playing tennis matches twice a week.

Good health is new for me. My health problems began in childhood. I remember having chest pain as a young child. I avoided strenuous exercise such as running. I became diabetic before age 10. I remember hearing the family doctor discussing "Richard's sugar problem" with my parents. As I aged, my health problems became more threatening. By age 60, I could see death waiting for me. My ailments included diabetes, digestive problems, prostate blockage, kidney failure, and pain in the heart and lungs. While my doctor realized how serious my problems were, he was not able to suggest solutions. I realized then why my elderly friends were so interested in their health. They weren't getting answers. I began to look for help elsewhere.

My healing started with a dramatic change in my idea, or

model, for how I could best help my body heal. The model we use when we treat our health determines whether or not we heal. That model is crucial. I grew up believing the Western ideas about medicine, ideas based on the materialist model, which is a simplistic idea of what a body "really" is. Western medicine views the body as a three-dimensional chemical machine that must be fixed by a specialist if it breaks. That often requires drugs or surgery. The conventional method is wonderful in the face of an emergency. However, it is almost useless in the face of the chronic ailments we associate with aging. If I had chosen to operate with the materialist model, my attempts to heal chronic problems would have failed and I would have died long ago.

Physicists seem to be a little more flexible in their ideas of "reality." For example, the number of dimensions in their models often differs. While three-dimensional ideas are very helpful when repairing your car's engine, they may not be the best fit for a discussion about body processes. For example, how many dimensions do you use when you ask how to cure a disease? Chemists and physicists see the world differently. Chemists look for vaccines or chemicals to help people. I am a physicist. When my life was endangered by disease, I looked for a physical not a chemical method to help myself.

In my present model, consciousness and the body are partners. Healing is the body's job. When dealing with a health issue, consciousness can help best as the body's assistant. The body, the true healer, must suggest a specific topic where consciousness can be useful. Then consciousness can focus—with the help of the body—on that problem. I can then apply logic, computer methods/technology, intuition, and scientific insight. The goal of consciousness is to help the body return successfully to its role as healer. I emphasize this point because it obviously violates the principles of the materialist medicine I grew up with. I concluded that many of the problems I faced in my youth were due to the materialist model I used then. In fact, if I still believed in that model today, none of the methods could help me now. Belief is key.

Healing required that I learned to ask simple direct questions that could be answered unambiguously by the body with a simple yes or no. These questions then were able to lead me to cures that otherwise would have been impossible.

My wife and I have been partners in healing since we made good nutrition a primary requirement in our lives: healthy fats, low sugar, organic vegetables and fruits, grass-fed meat, and wild-caught fish. In 1997, we discovered a brilliant healing method that gave us hope in *The Cure for All Diseases,* by Dr. Hulda Clark, who was impressed by the powerful healing she experienced as a result of using a frequency generator. Her work inspired me to attempt using frequencies myself, which gradually led me to building my own generators.

My physics background helped me here. I found it natural to think about using frequencies to improve my health since experimental electronic gadgetry had been part of my life for a long time. We started simply with Dr. Clark's "zapper." When I decided to carry this idea further, I began to experiment with inexpensive frequency generators that could provide safe high-quality electromagnetic frequencies. We had success in using frequencies for healing, but found that only your own body could provide the appropriate frequencies. We could not get them from books or from anyone else. I learned not to expect some "expert" would provide them. Similarly, we could not expect that our own frequencies would help cure other people.

While I admit I have no detailed information about how my body uses frequencies, it assures me that it does. I cannot pretend to truly understand the body's techniques, but I don't have to. I simply follow my body's instructions of how to help it use its own healing methods. It is important to sit in a quiet space to receive the information from the body about a good frequency to use. I enter that frequency for one of the generators to broadcast. Then I simply broadcast the frequency with a short antenna wire, so it is received all over my body. I suspect my body receives the broadcast frequency and its continued presence kills the organism. I am delighted to help with the task of making this a better place for us to work effectively together.

While this healing story I tell is my own, the lessons I learned about the body's healing abilities are universal. I believe that anyone can learn to work with healing frequencies. Before I could attempt to do any serious healing, I first had to become intuitive in a particular sense: I had to develop the habit of asking simple "yes or no" questions of my body. Many people do this instinctively. The Landmark Education courses I participated in for several years woke me up to new possibilities. In fact, it was at a Landmark class where I met my wife Elly. I was pleased with the new abilities I discovered in myself. Most important was the realization that my body can distinguish right from wrong. I adopted Dr. David Hawkins' method for communicating with the body (*Power vs Force*). When the body is strong, the answer to a question is "yes." When the body is weak, the answer is "no." I also developed the ability to read the body's energy through visualization.

In early 2010, at age 70, I became very ill and my wife forced me to see a doctor. I discovered that both my kidneys had totally failed. I was immediately put into dialysis treatment. My condition was very threatening. I was terribly weak and lay in a hospital bed for a month. At first I could not open my eyes for more than a moment. I needed a wheelchair after I left the hospital. I was unable to respond to a simple question from my wife. I quickly found myself spending 16 hours a week receiving dialysis treatment in a kidney clinic. I am very grateful for the help I received there. The staff at that clinic saved my life. However, my kidney doctor told me no one survives kidney failure. She said recovery from total kidney failure was impossible.

As soon as I returned home, I continued using the frequencies for healing. I questioned whether I would inevitably die from kidney failure, but felt quietly sure that I was recovering with the help of the frequency generator. As time passed, my health actually did improve. I recovered my ability to see and respond to the world around me. From there, I regained my physical strength and surprised everyone by getting back on the tennis court. Thanks to the frequency generator, three years after I started dialysis, I was able to walk away from it with strong kidneys. I had found another way to understand and treat the body.

Today, I combine weekly dialysis with frequency healing sessions and this method seems to have stabilized my health. Healing with frequencies has helped me so greatly that I continue to experiment with it. In particular, I have found methods to construct generators that are less expensive than the high-quality electronic frequency generator normally used.

All of my progress in healing with frequencies is based on

the premise that it is possible for me to decide what is best to do. My questions specifically involve improving the health of my body. Obviously the best source for this information is my body itself. Therefore I have learned to ask my body simple questions about my health and trust the answers it gives me. It is clear from the improvement in my health that the method works. I learned this skill late in life because I did not have it as a youngster. As a youngster I was helpless at cure, so I became good at coping. In fact, before age 60 I did not show any obvious talent for being intuitive. I want to emphasize that point here. If I was able to learn this skill so late in life, perhaps others can, too.

Chronic health issues point directly to the body's failure to accomplish its role as healer. The body is supposed to heal all the diseases that attack it. As I see it, chronic diseases are caused by the body's inability to remove toxins and parasites. People don't die of old age. They die of parasites and toxins. So many times I have heard people respond to their ailments with, "Oh, it is just old age." I think it would be more accurate to say that a person's health declines because the body failed to do its job: healing. If you intend to help the body heal, you must first learn to listen to it. Your body knows what it needs. Can you bring that knowledge into consciousness so you can get creative with the information? My wife Elly encouraged me to trust my intuition. She has lived her life by listening to "gut feelings."

When I began to work on the chronic problems of this aging body, my body and my consciousness had very limited experience communicating with each other. Over time, my body and my consciousness learned how to communicate. After all, the body and consciousness are partners. If consciousness refuses to listen, the body will not learn to talk. Likewise, if consciousness never talks to the body, it will not learn to listen. Both my body and my consciousness learned to communicate by attempting it and making mistakes. We learned from experience. There is much truth in Dr. Clark's model. I know that the frequency healing method has worked for others, too. The skill has saved my life. It has helped me produce cures in my body that medical professionals said were impossible. As you might imagine, the cures helped me to avoid some very expensive medical treatment.

It would be a healthier world if everybody could communicate with the body in this way. I recommend this form of learning. There is a big payoff. I am alive, I am in love, and my tennis game keeps improving.

—Richard Morrison, PhD

About the Contributors

Rosemary DeLucco Alpert is a master photographer based in Bellingham, Washington. For over 30 years, Rosemary has enjoyed taking photos of nature, places, and people and teaching classes. In 2016, Rosemary became the 70th Charter Member with Women in Photography International, and had the privilege of being one of Ansel Adams' last students.

Christa L. Armstrong is an RN specializing in Maternal Child Heath. Christa was introduced to Unity Church by her mother (a retired LPN), and carried it forward by becoming a member at Unity of Bellingham, Washington. Christa enjoys the loving people and the diversity of the community. Unity plays a pivotal role in her professional and daily life. Christa has two children; her first grandbaby will be born this year.

Aaron Buhler, a native of California, enjoys participating in the cultural life of Bellingham, Washington, where he has lived since 2007. He supports the music venues in the community and sings in the choir at Unity Spiritual Center where he is a member. Aaron also serves as a volunteer at the Bellingham Senior Activities Center, and enjoys writing stories and poetry.

Zella Chapman, born in Victoria, BC, Canada, discovered her special intuitive abilities as a small child. Musically gifted, she studied piano to become a concert artist, but chose a lifetime of service to others. In Bellingham, Washington, where she has lived since childhood, Zella started a foster home for end-of-the-road teens and volunteers for the Crisis Center. In 1990, she started the Santa Claus Crusade, providing food and gifts to elderly shut-ins, disabled Vets, and children, and hot meals to the homeless. Zella is the Director/President of Belwest Cat Rescue. She also serves as a chaplain and choir member at Unity Spiritual Center.

Kathy Chasteen loves to help people with their problems and make people laugh. Kathy believes that her true calling in life was to be a psychologist. She served as Director of the Chamber of Commerce in Ferndale, Washington, and enjoyed many adventures, including trips to Japan and hot-air balloon rides. Ferndale has a sister city in Japan thanks to Kathy. She has four daughters and three grandchildren, and found true love with her third husband, Chuck Chasteen.

Muriel Crusciola is a mother of three and grandmother of three. Muriel is happily retired and lives in Bellingham, Washington, where she grew up and raised her own children. She enjoys reading, meditating, and spending time with family.

Helga Deliban has dedicated her life to compassionate healing of body, mind, and soul. Helga is a "perpetual student of life whose life has been and continues to be a series of miracles." As a hospice volunteer, she is grateful for the gift in end of life care. Helga is committed to the Unity community and serves on the board at Unity Spiritual Center in Bellingham, Washington. She believes that expanding and growing our ministry is of utmost importance today.

Russ Eiriksson was born in Duluth, Minnesota, sandwiched between an older and younger sister. His father, a military career man, and his homemaker mom gave him a great childhood. Russ is employed as a real estate agent and also works in construction. Discovering the Unity Church in 1988, he enjoys the positive affirmations, loving people, and energy. Russ currently serves as Board President at Unity Spiritual Center in Bellingham, Washington.

Neal Engelking was born in Seattle, Washington, and spent most of his life in Phoenix, Arizona. After a three-year tour in the Army, Neal enrolled at Arizona State University, graduating with a B.S. in Psychology. From there, Neal worked in the sales and marketing fields, specializing in the residential real estate and mortgage industries. Neal is currently retired and enjoys his hobbies of country/western and swing dancing, hiking, reading, and blogging. To learn about Neal's mood elevating method, visit: www.AcceleratedStateConditioning.com

Moira Haagen centers her life in making an authentic heartfelt contribution. She holds an M.Ed. in Counseling Psychology and has worked with clients in the public and private sectors since 1992. Moira maintains a private practice as a Clinical Counsellor in Coquitlam, British Columbia, where she lives with her husband, son, and daughter. As a facilitator, she focuses on creating valuable learning experiences, with the recognition that each of us is unique. Moira is grateful for all the moments when she can say, "I love what I do."

Jonathan Hall is a clinical psychologist and dehypnotherapist with a private counseling practice in Bellingham, Washington. He holds a degree in Psychology and Clinical Hypnotherapy and was a staff member at the Woodbine Primal Center for over 12 years. Jonathan traveled throughout India and Nepal in the 1960s and '70s visiting ashrams and spiritual communities and was a founding member of the Findhorn Community in Scotland. He has taught meditation at Gonzaga University and Unity Churches for over 20 years.

Larry Harriman has had many interesting careers, the longest being buying and selling buildings and antiques. He and his partner traveled to England and countries around the world in search of fine antique furniture, especially clocks for their antique shop in Bellingham, Washington. They restored and lived in many old houses, including the historic 23-room Wardner's Castle in Bellingham. Larry now resides in a more modest home with his partner Eugenia and stays involved as a horologist. He serves as a chaplain at the Unity Spiritual Center.

Maureen Hofstedt feels blessed by the life lessons that teach her gratitude and strength. Her greatest gifts are her four beautiful children, and the further blessings of eight unique, very dear grandchildren. She serves as a chaplain at Unity Spiritual Center in Bellingham, Washington.

Bruce Hostetter has pursued multi-disciplines all of his adult life. Trained in landscape architecture and lighting design, he is passionate about design that inspires people in mysterious and intangible ways. With a love for creative writing and the mystical side of life, Bruce is always observing and listening, especially for the quiet voice that brings new insights. He is currently a student of transformative coaching at Invite Change in Edmonds, Washington. As a resident of Bellingham, he delights in being part of its many engaging communities.

Shari Humes lives happily at Sandy Point in Ferndale, Washington, with her husband Larry. She loves walking on the beach and creating art with shells and driftwood. Shari and Larry enjoy adventures on the water with their rowboat, kayaks, powerboat, and sailboat. They have a pop-up trailer for camping adventures. She and Larry have hosted an Abraham-Hicks study group at Unity of Bellingham since 2013. Shari is a Reiki Master. By blending their families, they have four adult children and five grandkids.

Dac Jamison, now retired from a great police department, says, Life is Good! He spends his time being a parent and grandparent, caring for dogs, gardening, teaching, hiking, volunteering, learning, and taking photographs. He loves his extended family, and his loving wife of thirty-five years keeps him pointed in the right direction. Dac cares about our environment and the impact we have on it every day. He is hopeful that peace will erupt soon and all life on earth will fruitfully coexist.

Kelly Jamison loves her family, friends, and Unity family. Her heart is bursting with gratitude. Kelly says she has learned more from her sons and grandsons than she ever taught them. She is a Reiki practitioner, now retired from a wonderful banking career. Kelly is a strong advocate for children, animals, domestic violence victims, a clean environment, and peace and love. She loves live theater, tennis, hiking, gardening, and everything outdoors. Kelly has been married for 35 years to the best man she has ever met.

Emma Jones, D.C.H., a retired counselor and program manager and agency owner, has worked in the fields of Mental Health, Substance Abuse, and Domestic Violence. Her work combines traditional psychological counseling, including cognitive therapy and NLP, with various spiritual traditions, Time Line Therapy, and Hypnotherapy. She is also a spiritual coach and teacher, healer, and artist. She has lived a life full of Miracles and is currently writing a book on her spiritual journey through this life.

Everyday Miracles

Joyce Jones enjoys taking care of people and helping them to love themselves. Whether it's the school children she is blessed to work with as a substitute teacher, or the elderly clients she takes care of, she puts her faith in people with a whole heart. She has discovered that life is meant to be happy and fun, with a satisfying variety of experiences. Among her joys are her four children, three grandchildren, line dancing, kayaking, biking, hiking, gardening, and learning how to live a fuller life from Abraham-Hicks.

Russ Kapp is living the good life in the Pacific Northwest as a professional jazz guitarist. His various writing contributions commenced in earnest following graduation from the University of Kansas with a B.A. in Anthropology. He has held numerous career positions in the writing and communications field, including twelve years with the nationally syndicated newspaper USA TODAY. His six-year stint with the U.S. Navy during the Cold War and the Vietnam Era remain a major influence on his efforts to promote world peace and harmony.

Ellen Bergh Kastler was born and raised in Oslo, Norway. She was 12 years old when Nazi Germany invaded Norway in 1940. The German occupation ended in 1945. After the war, Ellen stayed in Norway and worked a number of years. In her late twenties, she moved to the United States. Six months after her arrival, she met her husband, married, and became a U.S. Citizen. Ellen lives in Bellingham,Washington.

Kendra Langeteig, PhD (Editor of *Everyday Miracles*) is a writer and one-time English professor who reinvented herself as a book doctor for aspiring authors. Kendra is committed to shining light in new places and enriching the lives of others through books. The author of *The New Asian Home*, and the editor of many inspirational books, she is currently writing a collection of short stories. She lives in Bellingham, Washington. To learn about her editorial services, visit www.edgewisepublishing.com

Sally Legerwood believes that life is full of miracles every day—we just need to be open to them. Sally grew up in Washington and lives in Bellingham with her partner, a high-school classmate who she "re-met" and married. She loves hiking, fishing, and outdoor activities. Retired from a career as a massage therapist, she enjoys gardening, writing, painting, and fabric creation. Sally has been a Reiki practitioner for 35 years and a Reiki Master for 18. She teaches classes, sees clients privately, and conducts Reiki retreats.

John Wesley Logan moved to Bellingham in 1999 to be close to the mountains where he enjoys climbing, hiking, and skiing with his partner, 5 children and the Mountaineers. For over 40 years, John assisted people with tax, financial, and estate planning as a CPA and is now retired. He has been a member of Unity Spiritual Center for 15 years and facilitates *A Course of Miracles* and *The Way of Mastery* classes. John was born in Nashville, TN, where he developed his love of music. A talented singer, he graces the stage at USC.

RoseMarie Longmire grew up in Yakima, Washington, and raised her three children in Spokane before moving to Bellingham. She appreciates the beauty of the Pacific Northwest and enjoys outdoor adventures with her children and eight grandchildren. RoseMarie took a leap of faith in 2005, and created a new life with a career in real estate and has never looked back. Her passion is facilitating youth programs to encourage kids to pursue their dreams. Her latest adventures: becoming a licensed hypnotherapist and learning to play the piano.

Christina Lorraine's love of spirituality, nature, and the healing arts has offered her a very rewarding life. Today, Christina supports the Unity Spiritual Center-Bellingham as Director, and offers subtle-body re-patterning in her private practice. She also serves as the managing director for the Friends of Endangered Children Foundation, supporting the efforts of the Endangered Child Initiative. For information and donations visit: www.FriendsofEndangeredChildren.org.

Judy Milton spent her childhood surrounded by a variety of farm animals. These experiences proved to be defining moments for her work with animals later in life. She received a nursing degree from San Jose State University and was certified as a Healing Touch practitioner. After retirement, she became a Healing Touch for Animals practitioner to support animals energetically for self-healing. Skilled in animal communication, she connects with them on a deep level. Judy lives in Bellingham, Washington, and enjoys spending time with her five granddaughters and her Shih Tzu, Clair.

Everyday Miracles

Elly Friese Morrison, PhD, is a retired history professor and grant writer who immigrated to the U.S. in the 1950s. Her parents, Elly Scharnberg and Carl Friese, raised Elly and her three siblings in Hamburg, Germany. In 1942, they sent their children south to keep them safe from air raids. They returned to Hamburg in time to experience the end of the war at home. Elly's dream as a young piano student was to travel the world as a concert pianist. Today, she still enjoys playing the piano and sings in the choir at Unity Spiritual Center, Bellingham Washington.

Richard Morrison, PhD, is a retired professor of physics and engineering. Richard developed a method of working intuitively with frequencies that he has used for healing purposes since 1997. The improvement in his and his wife's health suggests strongly that this method is a powerful healing tool. He was able to recover from total kidney failure after several years of dialysis. Richard enjoys playing tennis, Hungarian folk fiddling, and singing in the choir at Unity Spiritual Center in Bellingham, Washington.

Erin O'Reilly, a bona fide Hamster, was born and raised in Bellingham, Washington. She spends time with plants, animals, three awesome sisters and wonderful friends. Now retired, she spends her time making "lotions & potions" for her WaterLily business. When not mixing it up in the kitchen, she sings with the choir at Unity Spiritual Center, and volunteers at the Assistance League Thrift & Gift Shop. Unity has been a constant in her life for over 30 years and has enriched it in countless ways.

Ross Osborne is a recovering appliance repairman who enjoys being outdoors, giving to others, and bringing new life to nearly anything not working. He's a drummer in the band Quiet Fire at Unity Spiritual Center, playing an eclectic mix of jazz, blues, and popular tunes. He is also a founding board member of the Whatcom Jazz Music Arts Center. Ross and his singing dog Louie live on four forested acres south of Bellingham, Washington.

Peg Rasband is a native of Utah and a mother of two daughters. Peg has worked in the corporate world for more than 40 years, has a B.S. in Business from the University of Utah, and a year towards her MBA at Westminster College, Salt Lake City. Peg also practices shamanism and is a skilled healer and transformation coach. While living in Bellingham, Washington, the gift of writing suddenly opened up and Peg surprised herself by penning a book! The short story offered here is an excerpt.

Beatrice Raymond loves the parks and nature trails in Bellingham, Washington, where she now lives. Growing up in the Pacific Northwest, she enjoyed camping and hiking in the Olympics and Cascades. Beatrice is a retired Marriage & Family Therapist after counseling for 30 years. She also worked in the travel business, and has visited Europe, England, Mexico, Alaska, Hawaii, Canada, and the Bahamas. Currently, she enjoys walking her dog, house and pet sitting, bird watching, and English country dancing.

Marcia Reimers grew up all across the United States before settling in Bellingham, Washington at age 18. She has raised two wonderful daughters and has four grandchildren. Marcia loves music, and has been playing piano, singing, and writing music most of her life. She believes the songs she writes are actually gifts from Spirit being expressed through her. In addition to music, she loves gardening and spending time with her family.

Polly Richter has a great love of nature. Growing up, she enjoyed camping, hiking, swimming, skiing, and traveling to national parks. Raised as a Catholic (though she no longer considers herself Catholic), she deeply appreciates sacred ritual, especially contemplative prayer and chanting. Polly began a meditation practice in her early twenties. She frequently experiences beautiful imagery when she meditates, and receives messages and assistance from ancestors, spirit guides, and angels. Polly believes that more and more people are gaining higher sense perception.

George Rounthwaite lives in Ferndale, Washington, where he works in real estate and construction. He recently designed and built his dream home.

Penny Sanford was born and raised in Bellingham, Washington, where she developed a love and appreciation of nature. She enjoys spending time playing in the outdoors with her current partner, two girls, and her dog. Penny has worked as a professional Physical Therapist for 25 years and now specializes in CranioSacral Therapy. This practice has enabled her to experience the miracle of who we are and our own innate ability to heal ourselves.

Bell Spence, a former Type A personality, dared to change, and now lives in greater peace and grace. She lives in Bellingham, Washington, and is a member of the Quiet Fire band at Unity Spiritual Center.

Jon Strong grew up in Alaska, where he enjoyed the great adventures flying his plane on floats in the summer and skiing in the winter. Hunting, fishing, camping, and an occasional round of golf were among his favorite activities during the endless summer sun. Jon now lives in Bellingham, Washington, where he works in public relations, sales, and marketing. His favorite days are spent with his wife Stephanie and their three young grandchildren. Weekends often include a trip to Seattle for dinner with their younger daughter and her husband.

Stephanie Strong, a native of Texas, moved to Anchorage, Alaska, with her family as a child. She grew up camping, fishing, and helping her family build a log cabin at their homestead. After college she taught elementary school, and later started a company designing and manufacturing girls' fashion accessories sold through Nordstrom. She also earned a degree in Interior Design, and is an ASID Award Winning designer in both residential and commercial design. She lives in Bellingham, Washington, enjoying her grandchildren and producing beautiful paintings on silk.

Bob Trask is a leadership trainer, spiritual teacher, and founder of the ARAS Foundation, conducting seminars in 13 countries for 30 years. Bob is now the Minister at Unity Spiritual Center in Bellingham, Washington. He brings to his ministry a lifetime of diverse experiences, including wilderness guide, scuba diving instructor, master sea captain, firefighter, EMT, actor, and singer. He is also the author of inspirational self-help books and novels. When not busy with his work, Bob enjoys time with his wife Mary and their daughter Chauncey.

Mary Trask, from the time she was a young child living in Missouri, loved lending a hand to someone in need. After graduating with a Sociology degree, she moved to the Pacific Northwest and brought with her that same passion for community service. When not involved with a community project, she loves to garden and curl up with her two cats and a good book. Her greatest joy comes from sharing adventures with her husband Bob and daughter Chauncey.

Alita Walton was born, raised, and lived most of her life in Bellingham, Washington. Retired from a career as a medical transcriptionist, Alita enjoys spending time with her kitties and her daughter. During the 1990s, she became a minister of the Universal Church of the Master. At the time, she also channeled and performed psychic readings. Alita was one of the early members of the first Unity Church in Bellingham. She now serves as a chaplain at Unity Spiritual Center.

www.ingramcontent.com/pod-product-compliance
Lightning Source LLC
LaVergne TN
LVHW011221080426
835509LV00005B/255